BATTLE OF THE BALTIC

BATTLE OF THE BALTIC

THE WARS 1918-1945

Robert Jackson

Pen & Sword
MARITIME

First published in Great Britain in 2007 by
Pen & Sword Maritime
an imprint of
Pen & Sword Books Ltd

ISBN 978 1 84415 422 7

A CIP catalogue record for this book is
available from the British Library

Typeset in Palatino by
Phoenix Typesetting, Auldgirth, Dumfriesshire

Printed and bound in England by
CPI UK

Pen & Sword Books Ltd incorporates the Imprints of Pen & Sword Aviation,
Pen & Sword Maritime, Pen & Sword Military, Wharncliffe Local History,
Pen & Sword Select, Pen & Sword Military Classics and Leo Cooper.

For a complete list of Pen & Sword titles please contact
PEN & SWORD BOOKS LIMITED
47 Church Street, Barnsley, South Yorkshire, S70 2AS, England
E-mail: enquiries@pen-and-sword.co.uk
Website: www.pen-and-sword.co.uk

Contents

Introduction

This work is primarily about the land, naval and air operations that took place in and around the Baltic Sea from 1918 to 1945. It begins with the naval operation prosecuted by the British immediately after the First World War, when the independence from Communist domination of the three Baltic states of Estonia, Latvia and Lithuania was secured for two decades. These operations were followed immediately by Poland's fight for independence, leading to further crises that, ultimately, devolved into the Second World War. That conflict had barely begun when Finland, in her turn, was fighting for survival in the bitter contest that became known as the Winter War.

Because this book is about military campaigns, I have not touched on matters such as the Holocaust and its effects on the populations of the Baltic region, nor have I mentioned, except in passing, the atrocities inflicted on civilians by both sides during the years 1941 to 1945, which have been well documented elsewhere.

Robert Jackson

The Geography of the Baltic

The Baltic follows a general south-west to north-east axis. The most significant stretch of open water extends from the island of Bornholm for some 500 miles to south-west Finland, where it divides into two branches – the Gulf of Bothnia extending 430 miles to the north, and the Gulf of Finland extending 300 miles to its head near St Petersburg, the former Leningrad. The average width of the Baltic is only about 125 miles and the average depth between 300 and 600 feet. Although the sea is practically tideless, strong north-easterly winds can whip up choppy seas, which can be hazardous for the navigation of small craft. The Swedish and Finnish coasts are heavily indented, with a liberal scattering of rocky islands, while the eastern and southern shores are characterised by dunes, sandspits, lagoons and estuaries. More than half the surface area of the Baltic ices over in winter, making the ports unusable without the services of icebreakers.

At its far western end, the Baltic terminates at the Jutland peninsula, at the base of which is the Kiel Canal. The Baltic drains into the Kattegat by way of the Little Belt, between Jutland and the island of Fyn (Fünen), the Great Belt and the Oresund, the waterway between Denmark and Sweden.

Prelude

The fog that shrouded the southern shores of the Baltic softened the angular lines of the great, grey battleship that rode at anchor a few hundred yards off the Westerplatte peninsula, at the entrance to the port of Danzig, where the river Vistula flowed into the sea.

She was a veteran warship. Launched at Kiel in December 1906, she was the last of the *Deutschland* class of pre-dreadnought battleships. Like

The veteran German battleships Schlesien *and* Schleswig-Holstein *(foreground) pictured at Kiel in the 1930s.* (US Navy)

her sister ships – the *Deutschland, Hannover, Pommern and Schlesien* – she had fought at Jutland and had later served as a tender and an accommodation ship at Bremen and Kiel. At the end of hostilities, with the once mighty German Navy reduced to the status of a costal defence force, she had become one the few battleships remaining in German waters, the rest having been surrendered to the British and later scuttled by their crews at Scapa Flow. Then, in 1925, had come rebirth: a year-long refit that saw her emerge as virtually a new vessel, followed by her commissioning as Fleet Flagship. She had served in that capacity until 1935, when the honour had passed to a brand new battleship, the *Admiral Graf Spee*.

Afterwards, she had slipped quietly into the role of cadet training ship. But the *Schleswig-Holstein*, for such was her name, was soon to be assured of a place in history. In two minutes' time, she would fire the first shots of the most terrible conflict in the history of mankind.

Her target, the fortress of Westerplatte, was of great strategic importance. It had been established by the new government of Poland in 1920, initially as a supply depot where military stores were offloaded, mainly from France. Poland, which had been partitioned between

The fortress of Westerplatte under bombardment by the Schleswig-Holstein *on 1 September 1939.* (Polish Ministry of Foreign Affairs)

Russia, Germany and Austria for a century, had emerged as an independent state at the end of the First World War, but fierce fighting had broken out almost immediately in the Lvov area, where the Ukrainian minority had attempted to establish its own government. During the months of warfare that followed, first against the Ukrainians and then against the Red Army, Westerplatte had grown in size and importance. A basin for discharging cargoes from ammunition ships was built on the site, as were nineteen ammunition dumps. A railway line ferried ammunition and other stores from these dumps to a railhead in Gdansk, as the Poles referred to Danzig, and in January 1926 a permanent Polish Army garrison was established on the site to provide permanent security.

In 1933, following the rise of the Nazi regime in Germany, the Polish government realised that Westerplatte was vulnerable to attack by German assault troops, should the somewhat tenuous political arrangement in Danzig break down.

On the bridge of the *Schleswig-Holstein*, Captain Gustav Kleikamp waited, according to the prearranged plan, to give the signal that would unleash a storm of shells on Westerplatte. He did not anticipate much resistance from the defenders, if any. The peninsula was defended by a garrison about two hundred strong, armed only with one 75mm field gun of French origin, two 37mm Bofors anti-tank guns, four mortars and a number of medium machine guns. There were no real fortifications, only several concrete blockhouses concealed in the forest that covered much of the peninsula. The garrison was separated from Danzig city by the harbour channel, with only a small pier forming a connection with the mainland.

In the event of war, the Polish garrison, commanded by Major Henryk Sucharski, had orders to withstand a sustained attack for twelve hours. No more could be expected of them.

Kleikamp was confident that surprise was on his side. The pretext for the *Schleswig-Holstein's* presence in Danzig Bay was that the warship was visiting these waters in honour of the anniversary of the Battle of Tannenberg in East Prussia, when the Germans had inflicted a crushing defeat on the forces of Imperial Russia in the last days of August 1914.

The Westerplatte assault force was in place. The first wave comprised one hundred and fifty Assault Marines, who had been hidden below decks on the *Schleswig-Holstein*; they had now emerged, and stood ready to scramble down nets into rubber boats as soon as the bombardment began. Once they had secured their initial objectives, they would be joined by reinforcements from the city of Danzig.

At 04.47, Kleikamp instructed his gunnery officer to open fire.

PART ONE

At War with the Bolsheviks;
The Baltic States and Poland, 1918–1939

CHAPTER ONE

Battle in the Baltic, 1918–1920

Almost exactly twenty years before the *Schleswig-Holstein's* main armament signalled the beginning of the Second World War, another bitter little naval conflict had been fought in the Baltic. The circumstances were very different, but the outcome was to change the future of the states that nestled on the eastern Baltic seaboard.

During the months that followed the October Revolution of 1917, the efforts of the Bolsheviks to establish Soviet control throughout the territories which had formerly constituted the vast area of Imperial Russia were intensely complicated – quite apart from the armed opposition of the loyalist White Russian Army and its foreign supporters – by the upsurge of nationalistic feeling and the move towards independence on the part of several states which had been under Russian domination for centuries.

Nowhere was this more apparent than on the eastern shores of the Baltic, where the states of Latvia, Lithuania and Estonia had begun a drive to achieve independence following the abdication of the Tsar early in 1917. Of the three, Lithuania had suffered most heavily from the ravages of war; the German armies had driven out the Russians in 1915, but not before the latter had burned and destroyed everything of value during their retreat. The Germans also occupied Kurland, or western Latvia, but the Russians held on to Livonia, the northern part of the state, and fortified it to resist a possible German advance on Petrograd, the name by which St Petersburg was now known (it would shortly be renamed Leningrad). Estonia was more fortunate; it was not until December 1917, following her secession from Russia in the wake of the revolution, that the Germans marched in. They completed their

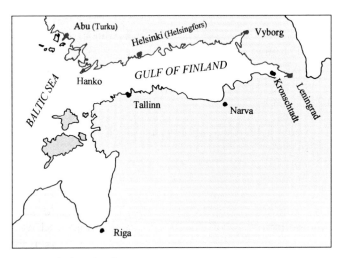

The Gulf of Finland

occupation of all three states in February 1918, when they resumed their advance following the breakdown of the armistice talks at Brest-Litovsk.

The broad German aim of turning the Baltic States into Prussian provinces died on 11 November 1918, with the end of hostilities on the Western Front. Among the clauses in the Armistice terms, Article XII stated that 'the Germans were to withdraw from the territory that was formerly part of the Russian Empire as soon as the Allies should consider the moment suitable having regard to the interior conditions of those territories. This meant, simply, that the German Army was to hold its position on the Baltic for the time being as an insurance against a Bolshevik attempt to seize control of the three states, all of which had been accorded de facto recognition by the Allies.

In practice, however, it was not quite so simple. The German forces of occupation in Estonia responded to the news of the Armistice by throwing away their weapons and demanding to be sent home. The mood was much the same in Latvia, although there was no actual mutiny as was the case in Estonia. In Lithuania the situation was somewhat different; there was no sudden and dramatic breakdown in discipline among the German troops, neither was there an immediate declaration of independence.

As far as Latvia and Estonia were concerned, it seemed that neither state would have much time to enjoy its newly-declared independence. Estonian independence had been reaffirmed on 11 November and a provisional government established under the leadership of President

Konstantin Pats, but within days a Soviet government was set up in opposition at Narva, near the frontier, and Red Army units began to advance into Estonian territory. By 10 December over half the country was in Russian hands. In Latvia, too, large areas were quickly occupied; the Reds had found their task ridiculously easy, since large sections of the population – and, in some cases, units of the German Army – were on their side.

On 13 November 1918, at a conference which took place in the British Foreign Office under the chairmanship of Lord Balfour, it was decided – as part of the British policy governing intervention in Russia – to supply the Baltic states with military material 'if and when they have governments ready to receive and utilise such material'. A week later, however, a delegation from the Estonian National Council came to London and pleaded for the immediate despatch of British troops and warships to protect their country; the speed with which events had taken place after the Armistice had given the Council no time to organise any effective defensive force, and the Germans still in the country would not resist the Red advance.

The Foreign Office pointed out that no troops were available, but told the delegation that warships might be sent. On 20 November, the War Cabinet agreed that a show of force was necessary in the Baltic to help deter the Bolsheviks, and that it would have to be provided by the Royal Navy. There were some objections, voiced by the Deputy Chief of Naval Staff, Vice-Admiral Sydney Fremantle. For a start, it would not be long before the Estonian port of Reval – the projected destination of the British force – was completely blocked by ice, which meant that any warhips sent there were likely to be frozen in throughout the winter. Secondly, there was always the chance that some units of the Red Fleet at Kronstadt, 180 miles from Reval, were still in fighting trim and might offer opposition; and thirdly – most important of all – the British force would have to negotiate the minefields with which the Baltic was liberally sown.

Nevertheless, the First Sea Lord, Admiral Sir Rosslyn Wemyss, gave his approval to the despatch of a naval force, and on 22 November the 6th Light Cruiser Squadron – consisting of the *Cardiff, Cassandra, Caradoc, Ceres* and *Calypso* – sailed for the Baltic from the Forth, escorted by nine destroyers from the 13th Flotilla and seven minesweepers from the 3rd Fleet Sweeping Flotilla. The force was commanded by Rear-Admiral Edwyn Alexander-Sinclair, flying his flag in the *Cardiff*. The ships' last mission had been to escort the surrendered German High Seas Fleet across the North Sea for internment at Scapa Flow in the Orkney Islands, and their crews – for the most part 'hostilities only' men – had been

Three of the light cruisers that sailed for the Baltic in November 1918: HMS Cardiff, Caradoc *and* Calypso. *The previous task of these ships had been to escort the German High Seas Fleet to internment at Scapa Flow in the Orkney Islands.* (Royal Navy)

looking forward to rapid demobilisation. Now, instead, they were being sent to some freezing, God-forsaken place where they would very probably be shot at. Needless to say, they were not happy.

Alexander-Sinclair's orders were to proceed to Copenhagen, and from there to Libau and Reval, where – apart from merely 'showing the flag' – his force was to cover the landing of arms shipments which were on their way to Estonia in the minelayers *Princess Margaret* and *Angora*. His orders made it clear that once the arms had been put ashore the Estonians and Latvians were to be responsible for their own defence; nevertheless, he was told that he could call upon the support of a squadron of battle-ships which was being sent to Copenhagen if he found it necessary, and he was also instructed to open fire on any warship operating off the coast of the Baltic provinces if it was thought to be hostile, without waiting for it to open fire first.

When Alexander-Sinclair arrived at Copenhagen , he found that the collier on which his coal-burning minesweepers depended had run aground and no stocks of coal were to be had in the Danish port. It was a serious blow, for it meant that the safety of his warships would now depend entirely on the accuracy of the route through the Baltic mine-fields shown on the charts. There was no time to wait for another collier; the Bolsheviks were already making rapid advances towards Reval and the situation was desperate. Within forty-eight hours, having been replenished by their accompanying oilers, the cruisers and destroyers were on their way again.

Off Osel, as the ships forged through the darkness in line ahead, disaster struck. There was a sudden explosion as the cruiser *Cassandra* hit a mine and began to go down fast, her back broken. Through super-human efforts on the part of their crews the destroyers *Vendetta* (Commander C.G. Ramsey) and *Westminster* (Lieutenant-Commander F.G. Glossop) came alongside the crippled ship in the long swell and succeeded in taking off over 450 officers and ratings – all but ten of the *Cassandra's* crew. They had been killed in the explosion and went down with the ship. The *Cassandra's* survivors were later taken back to England aboard the *Calypso*, which was damaged when she struck a submerged wreck at the entrance to Libau harbour. Two more ships also had to return: the *Westminster* and *Verulam*, damaged in a collision. All in all, it was not an auspicious beginning to the Royal Navy's venture in the Baltic.

The rest of Alexander-Sinclair's force reached Reval without further incident. The British warships arrived just in time to avert a disaster; the 7th Red Army was only forty miles from Reval, and the British commander realised that unless something was done quickly it would only be a matter of days before the town fell. He accordingly decided to ignore the Admiralty orders that virtually restricted his force to patrol duties, and on 13 December he sailed up the coast to Narva with the *Cardiff, Caradoc* and five destroyers. For several hours the warships bombarded the rear of the advancing enemy, their shells knocking out the only bridge across the river on the frontier and cutting the Reds' lines of communication from Petrograd; this, together with continual harassment by Estonian guerrillas, brought the offensive to a halt.

Alexander-Sinclair then sailed for Libau with half his force, leaving the remainder – including the cruisers *Calypso* and *Caradoc* – at Reval under the command of Captain Bertram Thesiger. On 26 December, at about noon, an unidentified ship suddenly appeared on the horizon and opened fire on the harbour. The vessel was in fact the Bolshevik destroyer *Spartak*, part of a small task force which had put out from Kronstadt to bombard Reval.

The destroyer *Wakeful* at once raised steam and gave chase, closely followed by the *Caradoc* and *Calypso*. The enemy vessel increased to full speed and turned towards the north-east in an attempt to break through to Kronstadt, but the Wakeful was faster and the range closed rapidly, the British destroyer opening fire at about six miles. The *Spartak* took evasive action and ran aground on a shoal, losing both her screws. The

The Russian cruiser Oleg *was prevented from bombarding Reval by the presence of British warships.* (Source unknown)

crew then hoisted the white flag and the British ships closed in; a boarding party was sent across, the Bolshevik crew formally surrendered and their ship was towed into Reval by the destroyer *Vendetta*.

From documents found on board the *Spartak*, it was learned that the Bolshevik cruiser *Oleg* was at anchor off Hogland; she was to have closed in to bombard Reval if the *Spartak* had encountered little or no resistance. Captain Thesiger, interpreting her presence as a definite threat to the security of his force, decided to attack her at dawn and put out to sea with the *Calypso, Caradoc* and *Wakeful*. At about 02.00 on 27 December the British warships passed what appeared to be a destroyer, which was showing no lights. Thesiger decided to leave her alone for the time being, but sent a signal to the *Vendetta* and *Vortigern* to put to sea and patrol the entrance to the Gulf of Finland in the hope of trapping her when she ran for home.

The British force reached Hogland shortly before dawn, but the *Oleg* had gone. Thesiger therefore turned back with the object of capturing the destroyer sighted a few hours earlier, the *Wakeful* sweeping between the *Caradoc* to the north and the *Calypso* to the south. With the warships spread out in this way, the hostile craft would not be able to pass them without being sighted by one or the other.

The plan worked admirably. The enemy destroyer found herself hopelessly hemmed in by five warships. Whichever way she turned she ran into either *Vendetta, Vortigern, Wakeful, Caradoc* or *Calypso*. After the British vessels had fired a few rounds the Bolshevik craft struck her colours and raised the white flag. She was the destroyer *Avrotil*. Together with the *Spartak*, she was later commissioned for service with the Estonian Navy.

Among the captured crews of the two destroyers – fourteen officers and 233 men – the British discovered a VIP; no less a person than F.F. Raskolnikov, Member of the Revolutionary War Soviet of the Baltic Fleet. Later, in June 1919, he was to be exchanged for eighteen British officers held prisoner by the Reds. The other Bolshevik prisoners were herded into a compound on Nargen Island, where forty of them were executed by the Estonians – despite British protests – in February 1919.

On 4 January 1919, the *Caradoc, Calypso* and *Wakeful* sailed for Narva to support a counter-offensive by the Estonian Army. The effect of the warships' combined shellfire was devastating. The range was less than 2000 yards, and with concentrations of Bolshevik infantry sharply defined against the snow-covered hillsides, it was impossible to miss. The shells hurled up columns of earth, snow and human debris in great, slow explosions and the Red infantry broke and scattered, vainly seeking shelter from the avalanche of fire and steel. As the Estonian troops advanced on the disorganised Bolsheviks the warships' guns laid a searching barrage on the enemy's artillery positions; there was no answering fire.

By the end of the first week in January, with the help of the Royal Navy, the spine of the Red offensive in Estonia had been broken and the 7th Red Army was being pushed steadily back. In Latvia, however, the picture was a great deal gloomier; here, a force of some 20,000 Reds continued to make considerable territorial gains, and because of geographical considerations Alexander-Sinclair's warships at Libau could provide no effective fire support for the flagging Latvian forces. To add to the danger, the German forces still in Latvia – about 40,000 men – had made it clear that they intended to evacuate the country as quickly as possible, leaving behind their weapons and war stores to fall into Bolshevik hands.

The Lettish Government, which had been forced to fall back on Riga, begged Alexander-Sinclair to land his Marines to strengthen the town's security, both external and internal. The Admiral, bearing in mind his orders, could not agree to this; nevertheless, some Marine officers did go ashore to organise companies of Lettish volunteers. Alexander-Sinclair also ordered the German High Commissioner and the commander of the German 8th Army to comply with Article XII of the Armistice terms. This would have meant that the Germans, in addition to defending Riga against the Bolsheviks, would have had to recapture those parts of Latvia already occupied by the Reds – an impossible task, considering the state of demoralisation among the German troops. The German commander, General von Ersdorff, insisted that he had been trying to obtain fresh troops from Germany since the previous November, but it was clear that he had no wish to order his men into action unconditionally.

Meanwhile, there was a rapid increase in Bolshevik activity inside Riga. The main Red force was now only twenty-five miles from the town, and the two Lettish regiments opposing it were in full retreat. Faced with the threat of a Bolshevik uprising in Riga the British began evacuating about 350 British and Allied subjects, and while this was going on – on 29 December 1918 – one of the Lettish regiments mutinied and the soldiers announced their intention of joining forces with the Bolsheviks. The Government turned to the Germans for help in putting down the mutiny, but the Germans refused and it was left to the British to take a hand.

On the night of 29/30 December Captain H.H. Smyth, the senior British naval officer in Riga, ordered the cruiser *Ceres* to open fire on the mutineers' barracks in the town. Within an hour the mutineers had surrendered and the tension eased a little, although serious outbreaks of violence were only prevented by the presence of British naval patrols ashore. These were withdrawn at 02.00 on 2 January, and at dawn the following morning the whole British naval force sailed for Copenhagen. Nothing could be done to save the port, which was occupied by the Bolsheviks on 3 January.

At Copenhagen, Alexander-Sinclair's ships were joined by the victorious detachment from Reval, and on 10 January they sailed for Rosyth. Meanwhile, in London, the Admiralty had been urging the War Cabinet to adopt a more definite and resolute policy in the Baltic. The Cabinet still remained opposed to the idea of landing British troops, but they recognised the need for maintaining a strong naval presence and agreed to despatch a force of two light cruisers and five destroyers to relieve Alexander-Sinclair's squadron.

The man chosen to command the replacement force was Rear-Admiral Walter Cowan. 'The primary object of your visit', his orders read, 'is to show the British flag and support British policy. The Estonian and Latvian Governments have been supplied with 10,000 rifles, together with machine guns and ammunition, by Rear-Admiral Sinclair. Any further supply should only be granted should you be reasonably convinced that the Estonian or other Government is of a stable nature and can control the Army, and that it will not be used in a manner opposed to British interests which may be summed up as follows: to prevent the destruction of Estonia and Latvia by external aggression, which is only threatened at present by Bolshevik invaders. The Germans are bound under the terms of the Armistice to withdraw from the ex-Russian Baltic provinces, and in no case should you have any dealings with them. Whenever we are in a position to resist Bolshevik attacks by force of arms from the sea we should unhesitatingly do so. A Bolshevik man-of-war or armed auxiliary operating off the coast of the Baltic provinces must be assumed to be doing so with hostile intent and treated accordingly. It is essential that you should not interfere with local politics, nor give colour for the assumption that Great Britain is favouring one party or another. You should be careful to raise no hope of any military assistance other than the supply of arms. No men are to be landed from your squadron unless under some very exceptional circumstances.'

The brief was, to say the least, vague and non-committal, and Cowan decided to interpret it in the only way possible. He would assess the situation in Estonia and Latvia, and then use his common sense in dealing with it.

Cowan's immediate destination after refuelling at Copenhagen was Libau, which he reached on 17 January 1919, flying his flag in the cruiser

Caledon and accompanied by three destroyers. The situation in Latvia was still critical; the Lettish Government, which had withdrawn to Libau when Riga fell, expected that the Bolsheviks would be in full control of the country by the end of the month. The Red drive was unexpectedly checked by a short-lived Lettish counter-offensive during the last week in January, but on 31 January the enemy advanced once more and occupied the port of Windau, forty miles from Libau. This brought a request for British help from the Lettish Government; Cowan sought Admiralty approval, and it was quickly forthcoming. On 9 February, he took the *Caledon* north to Windau and bombarded the Bolshevik positions in the town to such good effect that the Reds retreated.

Meanwhile, additional Allied naval reinforcements had arrived at Libau in the shape of the French cruiser *Montcalm* and two destroyers, and their presence – together with the effect of the *Caledon's* 6-inch shells at Windau – did much to raise the morale of the Government. Negotiations were under way with the object of establishing a common front against the Bolsheviks with Estonia, and the little Lettish army was growing steadily. Moreover, a new German commander, Major-General Rudiger von der Goltz, had arrived in Latvia; this was the man whose army had helped the Finnish leader Marshal Mannerheim to sweep the Reds out of Finland in 1918, and there were hopes that under the stimulus of his command the German forces in the Baltic States might yet rally to the anti-Bolshevik cause. By this time fresh German reinforcements had begun to arrive in some numbers, and once the build-up was complete von der Goltz planned to march on Riga. The Letts, however, viewed the growing German troop concentrations with some misgivings; they knew only too well that the Germans' motives were far more profound than was outwardly apparent, and that the old German aim of gaining control of the Baltic Provinces remained unchanged.

On 13 February 1919, the warships *Phaeton* and *Inconstant* of the First Light Cruiser Squadron, accompanied by five destroyers, arrived in the Baltic to relieve Cowan's force. The latter sailed for Rosyth a week later, leaving naval operations in the Baltic for the next few weeks under the command of Captain J.E. Cameron. With him was a small military mission under Major A.H. Keenan, of the Black Watch.

Cameron soon found himself with a crisis on his hands. Von der Goltz, who now had 12,000 troops under his command in Latvia, felt confident enough to challenge British authority, and when the Admiralty ordered that there were to be no further movements of troops and supplies between the Germans and east Baltic ports the German commander retaliated by halting the combined German-Lettish advance on Riga, which had begun on 5 March. He also threatened to withdraw his entire force, and the British War Cabinet now found itself in the un-enviable position of having to take full responsibility for the Bolsheviks overrunning the country if it continued to deny sea transport to von der Goltz, or of seeing the German 'police force' in Latvia turn into a fully-fledged army of occupation if it gave in to the German commander's demands.

There was an apparent way out, but it meant becoming more embroiled in Latvia's internal affairs than the Cabinet would have wished. It involved, in addition to meeting urgent demands for arms, war stores and essential supplies, the despatch of military and diplo-matic missions to the Baltic States. It was hoped that their influence would effectively break what was fast becoming a German stranglehold. By the end of March 1919 the German forces – on Goltz's orders – were living off the land, and in many areas the Lettish population had been reduced to starvation level. The British Government had arranged for a consignment of flour to be sent to Libau, but it would be the middle of April before it arrived.

Admiral Cowan, meanwhile, returned to the Baltic on 3 April with two cruisers and ten destroyers, bringing with him 20,000 rifles, six 6-inch howitzers, twelve 18-pounders and twenty lorries for the Lettish Army. Predictably, it was not long before there was a confrontation between Cowan and the German commander. Goltz would not commit himself to resuming the advance on Riga, even if the Allies were prepared to lift their naval blockade, and it was clear that he intended to resist the British efforts to assist the Letts in creating a sizeable army. On 16 April, without warning, a German battalion attacked the Lettish GHQ and arrested all the senior officers present, afterwards setting fire to the building. At the same time, several Lettish guards in the harbour area of Libau were also arrested.

The signs were ominous. It looked as though the Germans were plan-ning the seizure of the freighter *Saratov*, which was being used as a stores ship for the arms and ammunition supplied by the British. On Cowan's orders, the vessel's crew raised steam and moved her to a place of safety in the outer harbour, under the guns of the British cruisers. Meanwhile, a force of armed Balts – settlers of German stock – had surrounded the Lettish Government offices in an attempt to seize President Ulmanis and his ministers; Ulmanis and his Finance Minister, however, sought refuge in the British Legation, and two more ministers were rescued by the destroyers *Seafire* and *Scotsman*. A polite warning that the destroyers would open fire at point-blank range unless the Balts dispersed had the desired effect. Nevertheless, it could not be denied that the Balts' coup, although not as successful as had been anticipated, had achieved its primary objective; the Lettish Government had been rendered ineffective and had been replaced by a temporary military dictatorship.

Cowan immediately delivered an ultimatum to Goltz, demanding that the man who had led the coup – a young Baltic baron named Hasso von Manteuffel – be removed from Libau without delay, that Ulmanis be reinstated and his arrested ministers released. Goltz reluctantly agreed to the first demand, but he appeared to have every intention of stalling for time indefinitely on the matter of reinstating the Lettish Government; he maintained that Ulmanis and his ministers were Bolshevik sympathisers and that he would be failing in his duty to the Allies if he secured their release. While the wrangling continued, Goltz – although he later maintained that he had not been instrumental in organising or supporting the coup – worked hard behind the scenes to consolidate the Balts' position. With his support, a puppet Balt Government was quickly organised; it took office on 10 May and was headed by an obscure right-wing Latvian pastor named Andreius Niedra, a man entirely subservient to the German military command.

On 4 May, the Supreme Allied Council in Paris – whose order for the reinstatement of Ulmanis Goltz had openly defied – demanded that Berlin replace him with another commander and issue a statement to the effect that the German forces in Latvia were subordinate to Allied control. A few days later the German Government called Goltz to Berlin, but it was not to carry out the wishes of the Supreme Council. The Germans were in no mood to cooperate with the Allies over anything – they considered the Armistice terms harsh and unjust – and although they could not set the seal of official approval on Goltz's activities they were not prepared to forbid him categorically to proceed with the full occupation of the Baltic States.

Goltz returned to Latvia and immediately prepared to advance on Riga. At the last minute Berlin forbade him to use German troops, and the assault on the town, which began on 23 May, was carried out by the Landeswehr – the Baltic Militia – and a Lettish force under General Balodis. Goltz then ordered a further advance, not against a Bolshevik troop concentration to the south-east of Riga, but northwards in Livonia. Ostensibly, the purpose behind this was to allow Balodis's force to join up with other Lettish units fighting on the Estonian frontier, but the real reason was to provide the Landeswehr with a convenient springboard for a drive into Estonian territory.

Goltz's open defiance of the Allies had undoubtedly been made easier by the departure from Libau of the one man who could out-manoeuvre him diplomatically: Walter Cowan. On 25 April the British admiral had received a report that the Red Fleet had put out of Kronstadt, which was now free of ice; he had immediately steamed northwards in the *Caledon*, together with the *Seafire* and *Sepoy*, having sent out a signal for the cruiser *Cleopatra* and several destroyers in Copenhagen to join him with all speed.

On 7 May the cruiser *Curacao* arrived from England to relieve the *Caledon*, and Cowan transferred his flag to her. A week later, the new arrival struck a mine off Reval, but she was able to limp into port for temporary repairs and subsequent passage to England. Cowan was forced to transfer his flag yet again, this time to the *Cleopatra* – the only cruiser left under his command. The Admiralty had promised to send the 6-inch cruiser *Dragon* north from Danzig, but Cowan could not afford to await her arrival; he had already committed his ships to supporting an Estonian landing in Kaporia Bight that same day, 13 May.

While the Estonian forces engaged the Bolsheviks ashore, the *Cleopatra* and three destroyers stood off near Seskar Island. Since Kronstadt was less than forty miles away it was expected that the Red Fleet would try to interfere with the Estonian landings right from the start, but it was not until 17 May that any threat materialised from that quarter. At about 09.00 the British force sighted the enemy warships: four minesweepers and the destroyer *Gavriil*. Cowan immediately ordered *Cleopatra* to close with the enemy, together with the destroyers *Scout*, *Shakespeare* and *Walker*. At 09.45 *Cleopatra* opened fire at a range of 16,000 yards and the Bolshevik vessels turned back. Cowan continued the chase right up to the edge of the minefields protecting the approaches to Kronstadt, firing on the *Gavriil* until she pulled out of range. The British ships then came under heavy fire from the 6-inch guns of a Bolshevik shore battery, and when two enemy warships – the dreadnought *Petropavlovsk* and the cruiser *Oleg* – were sighted heading out of the harbour Cowan gave the order to withdraw.

The following day, the cruiser *Dragon* joined Cowan's forces off Seskar Island. The 23 and 24 May saw the arrival of substantial reinforcements, approved at long last by the War Cabinet under pressure from the Admiralty; they included a flotilla of 'E', 'H' and 'L' Class submarines under the command of Captain Martin Dunbar-Nasmith, VC, together with the depot ship HMS *Lucia*; the remainder of the First Destroyer Flotilla under Captain G.W.M. Campbell; three minesweepers, the *Banbury*, *Lanark* and *Hexham*; the fleet oiler *War Export*, which limped into Reval after striking a mine en route; and the cruiser *Galatea*.

The last-named ship brought Lieutenant-General Sir Hubert Gough. In March 1918 he had commanded the Fifth Army on the Western front, which had borne the full shock of the first Ludendorff Offensive. Now, over a year later, Gough had been given the task of leading a full British military mission to the Baltic Provinces. As well as reporting on how best the Allies might help the Baltic States in their struggle against the Bolsheviks, he was also to ascertain the requirements of the White Russian Army in the north-west; and, by no means least important, he was to break the German stranglehold on Latvia and Lithuania and bring Goltz's troops under firm Allied control pending their withdrawal. All this, however, was to be achieved without committing Britain to sending an army to the Baltic.

The minesweepers and submarines were at once set to work, the former sweeping a channel between Reval, Libau and Copenhagen and the latter patrolling the approaches to Kronstadt, a move that enabled Cowan to withdraw the bulk of his force to Reval. On 29 May, intelligence reports suggested that the Reds were planning an amphibious landing, and early that evening the Red destroyer *Azard* was sighted by the submarine L16, escorting six minesweepers out of Kronstadt. The submarine at once attacked the destroyer, but her torpedoes missed. Then an Estonian aircraft appeared overhead and released several bombs, one of which damaged the minesweeper *Kluz,* and the Bolshevik force returned to base.

At dawn the next day Cowan, determined to bring the Red Fleet to

British sailors cheer an E-class submarine (in this case the E11) *on its return from a war patrol. The E-class boats were among the most effective submarines of World War One.* (IWM)

action, sailed from Reval with the *Cleopatra, Dragon, Galatea*, the flotilla leader *Wallace* and five destroyers, anchoring off Seska at noon. The destroyer *Walker* and the submarines E27 and L16 patrolled the fringe of the Red minefields, and on the morning of 31 May they sighted several more minesweepers leaving Kronstadt, accompanied by the *Petropavlovsk* and the *Azard*. There was a brief exchange of fire between the *Azard* and the *Walker,* then the rest of Cowan's ships came up fast and the Red destroyer withdrew towards the *Petropavlovsk*. Both ships then retreated towards their base, shepherding the minesweepers, and the dreadnought's 12-inch guns laid down a barrage that was sufficiently heavy and accurate to prevent the British destroyers from closing the range any further. Once again, an Estonian aircraft put in an appearance and its bombs damaged the minesweeper *Zapal*.

There were signs that these limited sorties by the Red Fleet might soon give way to activity on a much larger scale. The 7th Red Army was by this time under heavy pressure from the White Russian North-West Army under General Rodzianko, who – despite the fact that the Reds had 50,000 troops opposing his 16,000 – was planning an early advance on Petrograd. This would be sustained by Allied supplies channelled through Estonia, and it was likely that the Red Fleet would make every attempt to send at least some of them to the bottom.

Realising the importance of bringing the Red Fleet to battle as close to Kronstadt as possible, Admiral Cowan decided to establish an advanced operational base for a British naval force. The site he selected was Biorko Sound, a large inlet on the Finnish coast only thirty miles from Kronstadt. The Finnish government raised no objection; in fact, they offered to place part of their own naval forces at Cowan's disposal.

On 2 June the admiral despatched some of his destroyers and two submarines to patrol the approaches to Petrograd Bay; he had to assume that the Reds might anticipate his intentions and attempt to mine the sound. There were two short and inconclusive engagements between the British destroyers and the Bolshevik destroyers *Azard* and *Gavriil* during the course of the day, and in the late afternoon the latter warship was attacked by the submarine L55 (Commander C.M.S. Chapman). The torpedoes failed to find their mark, but the *Gavriil's* gunners were more fortunate. One of their shells tore through the L.55's pressure hull and the submarine sank with the loss of all hands. In 1928 she was salvaged by the Soviet Navy and served as the pattern for a class of twenty-five submarines, also called the L-Class. The L55 herself, after repair, was commissioned in 1931 and renamed *Bezbozhnik* (Atheist). Accidentally damaged in the autumn of 1941, she served as a charging plant during World War II and was scrapped in 1960.

During these actions, the Bolshevik vessels had remained well behind their protective minefields. These were causing Cowan a great deal of frustration, and on the night of 9 June – when the *Azard* and *Gavriil* crept out to shell Biorko, then slipped back behind the minefields with impunity – the admiral made up his mind that something had to be done. He had no means of striking at the enemy in his lair with the cruisers and destroyers at his disposal; no aircraft had as yet arrived, and it would be at least three weeks before he was in a position to sow his own minefields with the return to the Baltic of the minelayer *Princess Margaret*. In the meantime, the Reds were free to launch a lightning attack on the British force at Biorko whenever they chose, and possibly with devastating results. The danger was stressed by Cowan in a signal to the Admiralty; in reply, the Admiralty stated that an attack on Kronstadt – quite apart from the technical problems – was contrary at this stage to the policy of the British government, and although it was not expressly forbidden it would at the very least cause great embarrassment.

It was at this point that Lieutenant Augustus Agar appeared on the scene. Agar commanded a detachment of two forty-foot Coastal Motor Boats (CMBs) based at Terrioki, a village near the Finnish border about thirty miles east of Biorko; their task was to run British agents across Petrograd Bay. The CMBs were admirably suited to the job; quite apart from their small size, which enabled them to slip past the Bolshevik forts under cover of darkness without much fear of detection, their shallow draught permitted them to cross the enemy minefields in complete safety.

Admiral Cowan, realising that the CMBs could possibly be used in a more offensive role than Intelligence work, had a stock of torpedoes – two of which could be carried by each boat – sent up from Reval, just in case the chance of action presented itself. It did. On 13 June 1919, by which time Agar's boats had made two courier trips across the Bay, the Bolshevik garrison of one of the forts defending the Petrograd approaches, Krasnaya Gorka, mutinied and turned their guns on the Red troops who were desperately trying to stem an advance by an Estonian force. Three days later, the C-in-C Soviet Baltic Fleet, Admiral A.P. Zelenoy, ordered the battleships *Petropavlovsk* and *Andrei Pervozvanni* to bombard the fort into submission.

The chance of neutralising both great warships in one surprise attack was too good to miss. On the night of 16 June, CMBs 4 and 7, armed with torpedoes, set out from Terrioki to attack, but the venture had to be abandoned when CMB 7 struck an underwater obstacle and damaged her propeller shaft. Preparations were made for another attempt the next day, but early in the morning the two battleships returned to Kronstadt.

A few hours later, however, they were replaced by the *Oleg*, which continued to shell the fort, and Agar – although the damage to CMB 7 had not been repaired and he had only one boat at his disposal – decided to attack the cruiser that night.

At 23.00 CMB 4 slipped out of Terrioki, manned by Agar, Sub-Lieutenant J. Hampsheir and Chief Motor Mechanic M. Beeley. The boat slipped through the minefield and past an enemy destroyer screen without incident; the dark bulk of the *Oleg* was sighted and Agar moved into position, firing his torpedo – in his own words – 'as if it were an ordinary practice run'. As the CMB turned away, the Oleg was shaken by an explosion and a thick column of smoke rose from her. With a gaping hole torn in her side the cruiser went down in just twelve minutes; amazingly, all but five of her crew were saved. The CMB, after running the gauntlet of heavy fire from the now thoroughly awakened destroyers and forts, regained Terrioki in safety at about 03.00. For this exploit Agar was subsequently awarded the Victoria Cross, while Hampsheir received the Distinguished Service Order and Beeley the Conspicuous Gallantry Medal.

Towards the end of June, more British naval reinforcements arrived in the Baltic; they included the cruisers *Caledon*, beginning her second tour in the area, *Danae* and *Dauntless*, which went to Commodore A.A. Duff's command at Libau, and the *Delhi*, which came up to Biorko to

The Sopwith One-and-a half Strutter formed an important component of Admiral Cowan's offensive air capability in the Baltic. (Source unknown)

relieve the *Cleopatra* as Cowan's flagship. More warships arrived in July, including the minesweepers of the 1st Fleet Sweeping Flotilla. Two of these, the *Myrtle* and the *Gentian*, were lost during subsequent clearing operations off Biorko Sound.

Perhaps the most important addition to Cowan's force, at least in terms of offensive capability, was the aircraft carrier *Vindictive*. A converted heavy cruiser of the *Hawkins* class, commissioned in 1918, she was armed with four 7.5-inch guns and, at the time of her arrival in the Baltic, she carried a mixed bag of twelve aircraft; Sopwith Camels and One-and-a-Half Strutters, Short Seaplanes and a Grain Griffin. Her passage from the Firth of Forth was not without incident; on the approach to Reval, on 6 July, she ran aground on a shoal at fifteen knots and was stuck fast for more than a week, in water three feet less than her draught. In the tideless sea prospects of refloating her appeared gloomy, even when she was lightened by some 2000 tons with the removal of fuel, guns and ammunition. It was not until a providential westerly wind caused an unexpected rise of water of six inches that three tugs, with the help of the *Delhi* and *Cleopatra*, were able to drag her clear.

By the time the carrier arrived at Biorko, work was well advanced on a rudimentary airstrip – little more than a 300-yard clearing in the forest – at Koivisto and a seaplane mooring at Sidinsari. After putting her aircraft ashore the *Vindictive* returned to Copenhagen, where she picked

The Short Seaplane, well proven in World War One, was used mainly for air reconnaissance. (Real Photographs)

The aircraft carrier HMS Argus *was used to ferry RAF aircraft out to the Baltic.* (Royal Navy)

up a fresh batch of machines ferried out from England by the carrier HMS *Argus.*

Operations by the RAF contingent, commanded by Squadron Leader D.G. Donald, began within a week of the aircraft being disembarked. Operational patrols were flown by the Camels, but no Red aircraft were reported in the vicinity. The Bolsheviks were not to have a substantial air commitment in the Kronstadt area until late in 1920, priority being given to the supply of aircraft to other fronts. Ironically, it was against their own former comrades that the first Red air squadrons to arrive in the Petrograd area were to have their first taste of action; it happened in March 1921, when elements of the Soviet Baltic Fleet mutinied and seized control of Kronstadt. In the space of a week, before the base was recaptured, the Red airmen flew 137 sorties against it.

The RAF aircraft at Biorko, during their early operations, were employed mainly on reconnaissance and anti-submarine patrol work. Admiral Cowan was seriously worried by the threat from enemy submarines, particularly after the night of 23/24 July, when one of them – the *Pantera* – made an unsuccessful attempt to attack British warships in the Kapiora Bight. Another attempted attack in the same area by the submarine *Vyepr* on 27 July was thwarted by the destroyers *Valorous* and *Vancouver*, which depth-charged her and caused some damage to the pressure hull.

The first major air attack on Kronstadt itself was carried out on 30 July, with the depot ship *Pamyat Azova* and any other submarines berthed alongside her as the primary targets. The aircraft involved were five Short seaplanes, three Camels, two One-and-a-Half Strutters and one Griffin, the strength being dictated by the fact that there were only eleven pilots available, and five of these were seaplane pilots. The two-seater Sopwith One-and-a-Half Strutters were flown off the *Vindictive* – which by this time had returned from Copenhagen with a fresh complement of aircraft – since the airstrip was still not level enough for use by machines carrying a full bomb-load.

The aircraft arrived over Kronstadt at first light and released ten 112-lb and six 65-lb bombs on the depot ship and neighbouring dry dock. The crews reported five direct hits and two large fires started. It later turned out that two of the bombs had dropped into the middle of a meeting of Red soldiers and sailors, killing and wounding over a hundred men. The depot ship disappeared from her usual position shortly after the raid and was not seen again. All the British aircraft returned safely, although they had to run through a heavy and accurate curtain of fire from the ships and batteries defending the anchorage. This was particularly unpleasant for the seaplane crews, as their aircraft would not climb higher than 4000 feet.

During August 1919, eight daylight and two night bombing raids were carried out in addition to the routine seaplane patrols, and several sorties were made against enemy kite balloons which were being used to observe the movements of the British ships. The Bolsheviks usually managed to haul them down in time, but one – over Krasnaya Gorka – was surprised by a Camel and shot down in flames. The enemy anti-aircraft fire, however, improved daily and balloon strafing soon became a hazardous pastime. In general, air operations were hampered by the inadequate airfield arrangements and by the condition of the aircraft themselves, most of them being old and completely unsuited to the duties they were required to undertake.

Meanwhile, Admiral Cowan had been working on a plan which, in its execution, he confidently anticipated would wreak so much havoc on the Red Baltic Fleet that it would no longer present a serious threat either to his own forces or to the left flank of the Estonian Front. The operation, code-named RK – the initials of Admiral Sir Roger Keyes, who had commanded the historic St George's Day expedition to Zeebrugge in 1918 – involved a combined attack on the warships by Squadron Leader Donald's aircraft and the CMBs, of which there was now a substantial force at Biorko. The idea was that while the air raid diverted the attention of the Red gunners, the CMBs would creep into the harbour, cut their way through the boom across the breakwater with the aid of explosive charges and then launch their torpedoes at their targets.

At 22.00 on 17 August, seven CMBs slipped out of Biorko Sound. At midnight they made rendezvous with Lieutenant Agar's boat from Terrioki. Agar's task was to lead them to the harbour entrance. Then, while one boat dealt with the destroyer *Gavriil*, the others were to concentrate on the principal targets: the battleships *Petropavlovsk* and *Andrei Pervozvanni*, the depot ship *Pamyat Azova,* and the cruiser *Rurik.* The latter was reported to be carrying explosive stores, and it was hoped that if she could be blown up she would take a sizeable chunk of the harbour with her. The position of all the enemy warships in the anchorage had been exactly plotted by air reconnaissance.

The bombing attack was timed to begin before the CMBs arrived within sound of Kronstadt, and was to last until they reached the harbour entrance. Individual aircraft were detailed to attack the guard ship anchored in the entrance, gun crews and searchlights on the breakwater, and to cover the withdrawal of the CMBs after the operation. All pilots had orders to do their utmost to draw enemy fire and searchlights away from the boats. All available aircraft – four Short seaplanes, two One-and-a-Half Strutters, a Griffin and a Camel – were to take part.

The aircraft approached the harbour from various directions, arriving overhead at 01.30 and releasing their small bomb-loads. The diversion was a complete success, all guns and searchlights in the harbour being fully occupied with the aircraft right up to the moment when the boats reached the entrance. Even then, a high proportion of the guns and searchlights continued to sweep the sky, and in fact some Bolshevik crews failed to realize that any British surface craft were present at all until the latter were on their way home. Having expended their bombs, sometimes attacking at mast height, the pilots went on circling over the anchorage to draw the enemy's attention away from the boats. One searchlight was put out of action by machine gun fire from a Short seaplane, while a Sopwith Camel made several low-level strafing attacks on searchlight and gun crews. One CMB, caught in the beam of a searchlight, was saved from a tricky situation by the gunner of a Sopwith One-and-a-Half Strutter, who knocked out the light with a short burst of machine-gun fire.

Under cover of the diversion the CMBs crept into the harbour at low speed, to cut down the engine noise and tell-tale bow wakes. The first three crews, who expected to have to blast their way through the boom, found to their amazement and delight that there was no boom at all and that their passage into the main harbour was unhindered. They immediately opened their throttles and roared towards their objectives.

CMB 79 (Lieutenant W.H. Bremner) torpedoed the *Pamyat Azova*, which went down rapidly, while Lieutenant R. Macbean in CMB 31 attacked the *Petropavlovsk*. Both torpedoes struck home and the dreadnought began to sink. The third boat, CMB 88 (Lieutenant A. Dayrell-Reed) went for the *Andrei Pervozvanni*, but on the approach to the target Dayrell-Reed was hit in the head by machine gun fire and his second in command, Lieutenant Gordon Steele, had to take over. One of his torpedoes exploded against the side of the *Andrei Pervozvanni*, the other ran on to hit the sinking *Petropavlovsk*.

Meanwhile, Lieutenant L.E.S. Napier in CMB 24 had attacked the destroyer *Gavriil*, but his torpedo passed under the warship and did no harm. A second later, the CMB was blasted in half by shellfire from the destroyer and sank. Another boat, No 62 (Lieutenant-Commander J.T. Brade), while on its way into the harbour, collided with Bremner's No 79 as the latter was racing for safety. Bremner's crew were taken on board No 62, which then turned to attack the *Gavriil*, but her torpedoes also missed and she too was sunk by the destroyer's gunfire. The other boats all returned safely to Biorko.

The raid had cost the British three boats, with four officers and four men killed and three officers and six men taken prisoner (they were repatriated in 1920). Dayrell-Reed's head wound proved to be fatal, and he died aboard HMS *Delhi* three and a half hours later. The raid, however, had been an immense success. Air reconnaissance showed that the *Pamyat Azova* and the two battleships had all been sunk, and were lying on their sides in shallow water. The threat to the British forces in the Baltic had been effectively removed; all that remained to oppose them was a handful of destroyers and submarines.

For their part in the attack, two officers – Lieutenant Steele and Commander C.C. Dobson (the CMB Flotilla commander, who had taken part in the raid in No 31) – received the Victoria Cross; Agar and three other officers were awarded the DSO, eight officers the DSC, and all the ratings received the CGM. It would be another twenty-one years before an enemy battle fleet suffered such a devastating loss in so short a time; the time then would be 1940, and the place Taranto. 'When England strikes,' wrote Finland's Marshal Mannerheim, 'she strikes hard.'

Despite the losses they had suffered, the Bolsheviks were soon to show that they were capable of hitting back. On 31 August, the destroyer HMS *Vittoria*, riding at anchor to the east of Seskar Island, was torpedoed by the submarine *Pantera* and went down with the loss of eight men, the remainder being rescued by the destroyer *Abdiel*; and a few days later, HMS *Verulam* sank with the loss of twenty-nine men after striking a mine.

From now on, operations for Cowan's force became fairly routine, consisting mainly of bombarding shore targets in support of the advance on land by the Estonian and Russian armies. On 14 August, with the support of General Gough, a North-West Russian Government had been formed at Helsinki, and its War Minister, General Nikolai Yudenich, had been appointed C-in-C of the Russian North-Western Army. Despite a flood of British equipment, including six tanks with twenty-two officers and twenty-six men under the command of Lieutenant-Colonel E. Hope-Carson, little or no progress had been made during the summer months by the White forces. The situation was further complicated by the fact that the Estonians were losing heart; they wanted some guarantee of independence before resuming the offensive against the Reds, who were putting out tentative feelers to them with a view to securing an armistice.

Squadron Leader Donald's aircraft continued to operate over Kronstadt fairly regularly during September 1919. By this time, there had been a marked improvement in the accuracy of the Bolshevik anti-aircraft fire; the guns put up an intense, systematic and well-timed barrage whenever an aircraft appeared, and Donald suspected that German gunners were being employed. Although conditions at the British airfield were continually being improved, with the erection of wooden hangars and personnel accommodation, both men and machines were beginning to feel the strain; the aircraft which had originally come out with the *Vindictive* in July were fast deteriorating and

The aircraft carrier HMS Furious, *seen here shortly after being fitted with a flight deck aft, also ferried aircraft out to the Baltic. Note the safety net rigged aft of the superstructure.* (Royal Navy)

badly in need of a major overhaul. It therefore came as a relief to Donald when he heard that HMS *Furious* had arrived in Copenhagen on 8 September, carrying replacement aircraft, but the relief was short-lived. When the aircraft arrived at Biorko they were all without exception found to be in very poor condition, and only one or two were fit for operational flying. Nevertheless, the arrival of the new batch of aircrew was very welcome.

Seaplane patrols accounted for most of the operational flying during September, but there were also five day- and three night-bombing raids, two attacks on enemy ships and a number of balloon-strafing missions. Camels were used for the daylight raids, as they had a greater operational ceiling than the other types, but even at 15,000 feet the anti-aircraft fire was very accurate and one Camel was shot down. Over seventy bombs of varying sizes were dropped on Kronstadt in the course of the month. The seaplane patrols were maintained during October, despite unfavourable weather conditions; three daylight raids were carried out against Kronstadt and there were three actions against enemy surface craft, including one in which two seaplanes fought it out with an enemy destroyer in a snowstorm.

On 14 October, the principal bombing target was shifted from Kronstadt to two fortresses which were holding up the left flank of the White Russian advance on Petrograd; more than 300 bombs were dropped in five days. One Camel was shot down, the pilot being killed; another was seriously wounded. A seaplane was also shot down, but the crew was picked up unhurt by an Estonian destroyer.

Weather conditions at the end of October were very severe, and great difficulty was experienced in starting the water-cooled seaplane engines. These difficulties increased in November when the temperature was rarely higher than twenty-five degrees Fahrenheit during the day and more often about sixteen degrees. Hot water poured into the radiator appeared in the form of icicles at the drain cock, despite the use of glycerine, and warm oil poured into the tanks soon attained the consistency of grease. Ice between the points of the sparking plugs was another great source of trouble, and even when the seaplanes did manage to get airborne their engines would not develop full power. Moreover, whenever the seaplanes took off the spray immediately froze, covering the controls with a layer of ice which eventually caused them to jam.

Ice was now forming rapidly on the Gulf of Finland, and on 25 November the airfield and seaplane base were evacuated, the aircraft being re-embarked on the *Vindictive*. A few days later, there was an unexpected warm spell and seaplane patrols were flown from the carrier until

11 December, when Kronstadt was reported to be completely frozen in.

During their five months of active service in the Baltic the RAF aircraft had flown a total of 837 operational hours. Of the fifty-five aircraft deployed, thirty-three were lost; three were shot down, nine force-landed in the sea, seven crashed while landing or taking off, and fourteen deteriorated beyond repair owing to the climatic conditions. Four pilots were killed and two wounded.

While Admiral Cowan's forces were fully occupied in keeping the Red Fleet at bay, General von der Goltz continued to use all his influence to resist the evacuation of his forces from the Baltic provinces, and in Germany the Weimar Government ignored Allied demands for the general's recall. During August and September 1919 volunteers of the Freikorps – German irregular troops – went on pouring into Latvia, where they were formed into a Russo-German force known as the Western Russian Army. This was commanded by Colonel Pavel Mikhailovich Avalov-Bermondt, a Caucasian adventurer who had been mixed up in German intrigues of one kind or another for some time. He had arrived in Latvia in June at the head of a force of volunteers recruited from among the large number of White Russian émigrés in Germany, and Goltz had not been slow to recognise his potential. Bermondt's appointment as commander of the Western Russian Army was an excellent way of overcoming Allied objections to the force being commanded by Goltz himself, and since Bermondt was firmly pro-German he could be relied upon to do exactly what he was told.

In September, there was a sharp increase in the already explosive tension between the German and Lettish forces, and unpleasant incidents multiplied. Lettish headquarters were attacked and looted, Lettish units forcibly disarmed, and Latvian and Allied flags ripped from government buildings. There was a steady flow of refugees from the German-occupied areas, where Bermondt's forces robbed and pillaged indiscriminately. In desperation, President Ulmanis sent a personal appeal for help to British Prime Minister David Lloyd George, stressing that the strife in Courland was having a damaging effect on the offensive against the Bolsheviks. The Allied Military Mission made repeated efforts to persuade Bermondt to join forces with Yudenich, but it was useless; Bermondt's plans envisaged a thrust into Russia from Latvian territory on Yudenich's right flank, but this had nothing to do with the strategic aims of the North-West Army. Instead, it was a clear attempt to expand the area already occupied by the German forces to include a large slice of Russian territory.

On 3 October 1919, the German Weimar Government, reacting at last to Allied pressure, ordered Goltz back to Germany and issued an order forbidding German units to recruit Russian volunteers. It was too late, however, to defuse the situation; Bermondt had no intention now of surrendering, and that is what compliance with the latest order from Weimar would have amounted to. He had already made up his mind to subjugate the whole of Latvia before his drive into Russia, and on 8 October he marched on Riga with some 15,000 German troops.

To reinforce the 9000-strong Lettish garrison, General Balodis was forced to withdraw a further 3500 men from the eastern front at a time when they were badly needed for Yudenich's coming offensive against the Reds. Bermondt's plan was to capture the two bridges across the River Dvina (not to be confused with the North Russian river of the same name), cutting off the Letts from Riga; once this had been achieved the main German force would storm the town from the south. The Letts, however, fought back bitterly, and a fierce four-day battle developed around the bridges. The Letts withdrew successfully into Riga and dismantled sections of the bridges; both sides then began a furious exchange of fire across the river, threatening the safety of the two Allied warships anchored there – HMS *Abdiel* and the French sloop *Aisne*. The ships moved their position, but as the battle spread along both banks of the river they were both hit by machine gun fire and shells burst un-pleasantly close. They finally anchored in the mouth of the river, out of range of the guns, and on 11 October they were joined by three more warships, the French sloops *Garnier* and *Marne* and the destroyer HMS *Vanoc.*

By this time the Germans had occupied the left bank of the river as far as the fort of Dunamunde, and as far as the crews of the Allied vessels could tell they appeared to be firing on tugs and neutral ships in the harbour. The following day, the *Dragon, Cleopatra* and *Princess Margaret* arrived off Riga, having been despatched from Biorko on the orders of Admiral Cowan. The admiral had also ordered his warships to intercept and arrest any German vessels they sighted in the Baltic. Eight were quickly rounded up, and several more were seized by the Letts in Libau.

On 12 October, the British destroyers, under the command of Captain Curtis, moved to an anchorage opposite Dunamunde Fort and were employed for several hours in embarking refugees and members of the British Missions for transfer to the *Princess Margaret*. The ships were fired on several times during these operations, but no damage was sustained. That night the commander of the French naval force in the Baltic, Commodore Brisson, arrived in the destroyer *Lestin* and took charge of subsequent naval operations off Riga. His first act, with the authority of Admiral Cowan and the British Admiralty, was to demand the with-drawal of the German forces from their positions in and around

Dunamunde by 12.00 on 15 October. The Germans ignored the ultimatum, and fifteen minutes after the expiry of the deadline Brisson ordered the Anglo-French force to open fire. Within half an hour the Germans broke and ran, pursued by Lettish infantry and the 6-inch shells of the *Dragon* and *Cleopatra*.

Bermondt's first attempt to take Riga had ended in failure, but the fighting was by no means over. On 17 October HMS *Dragon* was hit four times by enemy shells, killing nine of her crew and wounding four, and on 23 October shellfire from well-camouflaged guns burst around the destroyer *Venturous*, wounding two men. The Allied flotilla carried out an intensive bombardment of the shore areas where the enemy batteries were thought to be located the next day, and by nightfall there was no more firing from the German side.

The respite brought by the guns of the Allied warships enabled General Balodis to redeploy his forces for a counter-attack. On 3 November, supported by naval gunfire, the Letts advanced. Fighting determinedly they pushed Bermondt's forces steadily back, and within a week the enemy retreat had turned into a rout.

On 4 November, while bitter fighting still raged around Riga, German forces launched an attack on the comparatively small Lettish garrison at Libau. This assault was also broken with the help of naval gunfire from the British warships *Phaeton, Dauntless, Winchester, Whitley, Valorous* and *Wryneck*; so were further attempts made during the next three days. On 8 November the British naval force received an important addition in the shape of the monitor HMS *Erebus*, whose massive 15-inch guns were soon in action. Four days later, after fierce fighting on the outskirts of the town, the German forces were in full retreat, streaming across the countryside with the Letts in hot pursuit. The *Erebus* continued to pound the enemy with her main armament up to a range of twenty miles. On 18 November, exhausted and in desperation, the Germans asked for an armistice. Balodis refused to listen, and his forces continued to harry the retreating enemy mercilessly. By the end of the month, the last German troops had been swept from Latvian soil.

The rout of the Germans meant that Balodis was now free to transfer a large part of his forces back to the Eastern Front in support of Yudenich, but it was too late. By this time, the Russian North-Western Army had staked everything in a last desperate drive on Petrograd, and it had lost.

The White advance, by 40,000 troops under the operational command of General Rodzianko, began well, with Cowan's warships and the six tanks of the British detachment lending effective support in the initial stages. By 21 October the Whites were only eight miles from Petrograd and Estonian forces were attempting to capture Krasnaya Gorka. Several

Red counter-attacks were smashed by naval gunfire and, in an attempt to prevent Cowan's ships from coming in close enough to break up subsequent attacks, the Baltic Fleet was requested to lay a mine barrier running westward from Cape Dolgy Nos. The four destroyers detailed for the job, the *Gavriil, Azard, Konstantin* and *Svoboda*, sailed from Kronstadt before dawn on 21 October. Three miles off Cape Dolgy Nos they ran into a minefield laid by Cowan's forces several weeks earlier. Three great explosions thundered out into the darkness, and within minutes only a mass of debris floating on the icy waters marked the graves of the *Gavriil, Konstantin* and *Svoboda*. There were no survivors.

On land, the Reds threw everything they had into the defence of Petrograd, with men of the Red Fleet playing a prominent role. The last-minute injection of 11,000 Red sailors into the line at Peterhof saved the crumbling Seventh Red Army from defeat and stemmed Yudenich's advance. Russian warships on the Neva, most of them unseaworthy but with serviceable guns, hammered away at the White Russian positions by day and night; and the Estonians, hopelessly bogged down in front of Krasnaya Gorka, were showing signs of demoralisation. It was at this point that the *Erebus*, which had been supporting the North Russian evacuation at Archangel, joined Cowan's force, and along with the cruisers *Delhi* and *Dunedin* she was used to bombard Krasnaya Gorka. Comparatively few shells hit the fortress, however, and the garrison held out. The monitor carried out a more successful bombardment on 31 October, but this was not followed up by any infantry assault.

Early in November, Yudenich announced that he was unable to continue with his advance on Petrograd; his army had spent itself. The Estonians, too, announced their intention of abandoning the attack on Krasnaya Gorka.

Then the Bolsheviks counter-attacked, and on 14 November they inflicted a crippling defeat on Yudenich's forces at Yemburg. The survivors streamed back over the Estonian border in disarray, many of them suffering from typhus. Here in the north-west, as in Siberia and the south, the spectre of defeat wore the same grim countenance.

Early in December, the Estonians, whose retreat from the Petrograd area had been made in fairly good order, covered by the guns of the British warships, began peace talks with the Bolsheviks with the object of securing Soviet recognition of their independence claims. One of the conditions laid down by the Bolsheviks was that all units of Yudenich's North-West Army on Estonian territory should be immediately disarmed and interned; this presented no serious problem, for the North-West Army had already ceased to exist as a coherent fighting force.

On 18 December 1919, with ice spreading rapidly through the Gulf of

Finland, Admiral Cowan evacuated Biorko Sound and withdrew his forces to Reval, sending a number of vessels – including the submarines – back to Britain. Ten days later, with no prospect of any further Soviet naval activity until the spring and the withdrawal of the last German forces from the Baltic States well under way, Cowan himself sailed for England with the *Delhi, Dragon* and the 1st Destroyer Flotilla, leaving the cruiser *Dunedin* and half the 4th Destroyer Flotilla in the Gulf of Finland.

On 2 February 1920, Estonia signed a formal peace treaty with the Soviet Government. Lithuania and Latvia followed suit on 30 June and 11 August respectively. The Admiralty anticipated further trouble from the Red Fleet in the spring of 1920, when the ice melted, and further reinforcements, including the battlecruisers HMS *Hood* and HMS *Tiger,* were ordered out to the Baltic; but on the last day of March the British Cabinet ordered all naval forces in the Baltic to abstain from further offensive action against the Reds, and a few weeks later the battlecruisers were recalled from Copenhagen. After that, the naval force was progressively reduced until only one light cruiser and two destroyers remained, and they too were withdrawn in 1920.

The naval war against the Bolsheviks was over. During the operations in the Baltic, the Royal Navy had employed 238 vessels of all types; losses amounted to one submarine, two destroyers, two minesweepers, seven CMBs and a store carrier, with 127 officers and men killed or missing. Twenty-six French, fourteen American and two Italian ships had also served under Admiral Cowan's command at one time or another, although only the French vessels had seen action alongside the British.

Admiral Cowan's had not been an easy command. His men had laboured under severe hardship, their already difficult task further complicated by outbreaks of mutiny and the effects of Red propaganda on war-weary minds. Yet they had done their duty; they had played an unforgettable part in securing the liberty of the Baltic States, so discharging to the full the role originally allotted to them.

Elsewhere, however, affairs had been set in motion that would one day determine the future of the Baltic lands, and change the map of Europe forever.

CHAPTER TWO

Poland: Birth of a Nation

In July 1919, the treaty that changed the face of Europe at Versailles brought into existence a new Independent state: Poland, which for a century had been partitioned between Russia, Germany and Austria-Hungary. Prior to independence, the small Polish army was involved in heavy fighting against with the Ukrainians; hostilities began in the Lvov area, where the Ukrainian minority had attempted to set up its own government.

In May 1919, an army of about 35,000 men, raised and equipped in France during the World War and commanded by General Jozef Haller, arrived in Poland, and with these reinforcements the Poles launched a major offensive against the Ukrainians in Galicia and drove them back

across the River Zbrucz. The Ukrainian forces under General Bredov counter-attacked, but they lacked real impetus and a further Polish offensive on 15 July resulted in the occupation of the whole of Galicia. The Poles then drove on into Byelorussia, capturing Minsk on 8 August and advancing on Berisov and Bobruisk. Later in August

General Jozef Haller, who raised and commanded the embryo Polish Army in 1919.
(National Museum, Warsaw)

Marshal Jozef Pilsudski, Poland's first head of state and founder of her armed forces, had earlier served five years in a Russian prison camp in Siberia.
(National Museum, Warsaw)

Marshal Pilsudski, the Polish leader, concluded an armistice with the Ukrainian nationalist Simon Petlyura; the latter had little alternative, since at that time his forces were fighting the Bolsheviks and the Volunteer Army as well as the Poles.

Pilsudski's intention, once his country gained its independence, was to re-create the boundaries of the 'Greater Poland' of the eighteenth century, a territory that included the Ukraine and Lithuania. The relatively easy conquests of July and August 1919 lent considerable encouragement to his plans; at the same time, policing the occupied area taxed the Polish forces to their absolute limit, and it was clear that before further expansion could take place – with the probability of hard fighting against well-organised Bolshevik forces – the Poles would need large quantities of supplies, equipment and ammunition. These could be acquired from one source only: the western Allies.

Pilsudski's stratagem hinged on convincing the Allies that Poland's newly-acquired territories would provide an ideal springboard for renewed intervention against the Bolsheviks. It was a possibility that had already been suggested to the French government several times by Marshal Foch, and rejected equally as often. Yet it was not to France that the Poles made their request, but Britain. On 14 September 1919, the Polish Prime Minister, Paderewski, offered Lloyd George an army of half a million men for a march on Moscow in exchange for a grant of £600,000 sterling to buy the necessary stores and ammunition. However, Winston Churchill pointed out that there was nothing to prevent the Poles from pocketing the funds and then failing to carry out their part of the bargain, or for that matter of concluding a separate peace with the Bolsheviks, and the offer was rejected.

Nevertheless, by the end of 1919 the collapse of the White forces in South Russia brought about a drastic reappraisal of Allied policy. On 8 December the British Ambassador in Warsaw, Sir Horace Rumbold, told Lord Curzon that in his view it would be better to supply war stores to the Poles instead of to the rapidly disintegrating Russian Loyalists, and four days later Lloyd George and French Prime Minister Georges Clemenceau agreed to transfer Allied aid to Poland now that the Loyalist caused appeared irrevocably lost.

Although both the French and British sent military missions to Poland – the former headed by General Henrys and the latter by General Alfred Knox – it was the French who retained the dominant interest in the Polish question and who supplied, ultimately, by far the greater part of the war stores. A steady flow of supplies did not really begin until the middle of January 1920, and even then the majority of the war material was Austrian war surplus, some of which had been stockpiled in Romania. However, it enabled Pilsudski to build up the strength of his forces substantially during the winter months.

One of the most important contributions made by the French to the Polish armed forces during the winter of 1919–10 was the supply of combat aircraft. The Poles had, in fact, begun to create the nucleus of an air force in October 1918, when the 1st Aviation Unit of the Polish Army was formed at Odessa with French help; this however was not transferred to Poland until the middle of 1919, and in the meantime – in

October and November 1918 – more squadrons were formed on Polish territory with the aid of some 200 aircraft left behind by the German and Austrian forces of occupation. These saw extensive action against the Ukrainians in the spring and summer of 1919, and in May of that year they were joined by seven more squadrons,

Captain Merian C. Cooper, formerly of the 94th Squadron of the United States Air Service, flew and fought with the 7th Squadron, Polish Air Force.
(National Museum, Warsaw)

One of the types used by the Polish Air Force in its early days was the German Albatros Scout, pictured here. (Author's collection)

equipped with French aircraft and manned by French crews, which arrived in Poland with General Haller's army. The French personnel were progressively withdrawn as more Polish airmen became qualified to fly the French machines, although a number stayed on in an advisory capacity – which did not prevent them, on occasion, from flying in combat.

In October 1919 ten American airmen joined the Polish 7th Squadron near Lvov. All volunteers, they were commanded by Captain Merian C. Cooper and included such celebrated pilots as Major Cedric E. Fauntleroy, who had flown with Eddie Rickenbacker's 94th Squadron on the Western Front. Seven more Americans arrived within a few weeks and converted to their new aircraft – a process that caused some amusement among the Western Front veterans, for the squadron was equipped with former German Albatros fighters.

Meanwhile, the Bolsheviks – in a conciliatory mood after their victories over the White Russian commanders Admiral Kolchak and General Denikin, and badly in need of resting their armies – had been making determined efforts to persuade the Poles to take part in peace negotiations. When diplomatic moves to this end failed, the Reds launched a series of small attacks along their western front; the Poles beat them off and held their positions. Throughout February and March 1920 Pilsudski went on building up his military strength for a counter-offensive against the Bolsheviks, despite warnings from the Supreme Allied Council that there would be no support for any aggressive move by the Poles against the Reds or, for that matter, against anyone else.

When the offensive did come, however, despite the ominous signs of the preceding weeks, it took the Allies completely by surprise. On 24 April 1920, Pilsudski signed a treaty with Simon Petlyura under which the Ukrainians were to be granted independence in return for military help in crushing the Bolsheviks, and on the following day, with Pilsudski himself in command, four Polish field armies smashed their way into the Ukraine, and by 7 May the Poles had occupied Kiev.

The embryo Polish Air Force played a vital part in the initial rapid advance. When the offensive began the Poles had about 150 combat aircraft, half of them serviceable; these were organised into three Wings under the command of Colonel Perini and soon proved their worth in a

The French General Maxime Weygand, seen here in 1940, was a leading member of the Allied military mission sent to Poland to boost morale in 1920.
(Radio Times Hulton)

series of devastating attacks on enemy armoured trains and troop convoys on the Dnieper. Then, on 15 may, the Bolsheviks struck back with a rapid thrust in the Potock area, and on 25 May they launched a general offensive all along the front. The treaty with Petlyura quickly proved to be worthless; the Ukrainians soon gave up the struggle and the Poles, outflanked by the Red armies, were forced to retreat.

On 10 June, Kiev was evacuated by the Polish forces and the Bolsheviks marched in. That same day the Polish Cabinet resigned; it was to be two weeks before a new government was formed. In the meantime, Poland was in political turmoil; the military reverses created widespread panic in Warsaw, and many factions pressed for immediate peace negotiations with the Bolsheviks. Others – including Pilsudski – made repeated approaches to the Allies in the hope that they would turn the tide either by direct intervention or an increase in military aid. The British, who already had contact with the Bolsheviks, promised to do what they could on the diplomatic level, while the French endeavoured to step up the flow of war supplies. Getting war stores through to Poland was not easy; munitions trains had to pass through Czechoslovak territory, and several were held up by the Czech railway authorities. To try to solve at least some of the problems and to boost Polish morale, the Supreme Allied Council sent a top-level mission headed by Lord d'Abernon and General Weygand out to Warsaw in July.

On 17 July the Reds crossed into Polish territory and began their advance on Warsaw. By this time the equipment situation of the Polish forces was critical, particularly in the air; only about thirty airworthy machines could be scraped together. The Polish squadrons had suffered heavily from ground fire during the general retreat in June, and the 7th Squadron was no exception. In May, the American pilots had exchanged their German machines for twelve brand new Italian-built Ansaldo Balilla single-seat fighters, but by 12 June only two were left. The remainder had been either accidentally destroyed or damaged beyond repair through enemy action. Twelve more Balillas were received early in July and the squadron was soon back in action, attacking General Budyonny's cavalry divisions which were spearheading the drive on Warsaw. The original batch of American pilots had now been joined by six more; one of them, Kenneth M. Murray, arrived with his own personal Sopwith Camel.

During the last week of July the Poles established a defensive line of sorts, and Pilsudski made preparations for a counter-attack with all available resources. General Weygand was opposed to such a move; he warned General Rozwadowski, the Polish Chief of Staff, that to launch a counter-offensive without first establishing a strong defensive line and

General Semyon Budyonny's Cossack cavalry led the attack on Warsaw, and suffered heavy losses to Polish air attack.
(Source unknown)

providing adequate reserves would be committing military suicide. Rozwadowski, however, had no real control over the conduct of Poland's military strategy. This lay entirely in the hands of Pilsudski, and the latter had no time for what he considered to be Western Front tactics. He believed that the best way to defend Warsaw was not to create strong defensive lines around the city, but to strike the enemy hard with everything at his disposal. As events were to prove, he was right; surprise and mobility were the key ingredients of Polish success. A static war of attrition would have been fatal.

At the beginning of August, the eagerly awaited fresh supplies of French and British war stores began to arrive in Poland. In addition to rifles, machine guns and ammunition, they included a number of Renault tanks and armoured cars. The material also included new combat aircraft, the first of 400 to be supplied to Poland by France, Britain and Italy during the remainder of 1920. France's contribution was seventy Breguet XIV light bombers, forty Spad XIII and fifty Spad VII fighters; Italy sent eight Salmson S.2A observation aircraft and thirty-five Balillas; Britain supplied 105 Bristol Fighters and – as a personal gift to the Polish Government from King George V – twelve DH.9s, ten Sopwith Camels and six Sopwith Dolphins. Thirty-eight Albatros D.IIIs and twenty Fokker D.VIIs were also acquired from German and Austrian surplus stocks.

There was no time for the Polish pilots to become accustomed to their new machines. They were taken into combat as soon as they were assembled, often by pilots who had never flown them before. The accident rate was fearful, and many machines fell victim to insurmountable problems of maintenance. Nevertheless, when Pilsudski's counter-offensive was launched in the Deblin sector on 16 August, every available aircraft was thrown into action in support of the ground forces, and under the combined air-ground onslaught the Reds wavered and broke. The Polish airmen were left almost entirely free to devote themselves to ground attack work; although the Reds had about 170 aircraft strung out along the front, they were rarely seen. When the Red airmen did put in an appearance, they usually dropped propaganda leaflets instead of bombs.

By 22 August the Polish spearheads had reached the River Narew, cutting off General Tukhachevsky's 4th Red Army from the bulk of the Soviet forces. Five days later the 4th Red Army was little more than a disorganised rabble, fleeing in disorder after a shattering defeat inflicted on it by the Poles at Grodno-Wolkowsysk. Meanwhile the Poles and the Bolsheviks, mainly as a result of British diplomatic initiative, had at last begun peace talks at Minsk. Earlier, with their forces at the gates of Warsaw and the capture of the city apparently a foregone conclusion, the Reds had tried to delay the talks – but now, with their armies in the field reeling back in defeat, they were only too willing to negotiate. Even so, in the early stages, the talks – which began on 17 August – progressed very slowly; both sides awaited fresh news from the battle areas before giving way on various points, and intelligence on the course the war was taking trickled through with considerable delays. It was not until 2

One of the most valuable assets delivered to Poland in 1920 was the excellent Breguet XIV, one of the finest light bombers to emerge from World War One. (ECP Armées)

September that the full extent of the Bolshevik defeat was known to the negotiators. The focus of negotiation then switched to Riga, and it was there, on 18 October 1920, that a peace treaty formally brought the Russo-Polish war to an end.

By the end of the year the majority of Pilsudski's Allied advisers had been withdrawn. Later, historians would name General Weygand as the mastermind behind the Polish military success, but the truth is that Weygand, apart from assessing Poland's military needs and advising his government accordingly, played no part in it. The Poles acted contrary to Weygand's wishes; the initiative was Pilsudski's alone, and it brought victory.

If credit for the Polish success must fall at least in part to the Allies, then it must go not to the generals, but to the officers and men, French, British, Italian and American, who devoted themselves wholeheartedly to aiding the Poles in building an efficient fighting machine; instructors, technicians, engineers and, above all, pilots.

The American volunteers were among the last Allied personnel to leave Polish soil; their demobilisation was completed in May 1921. Between April and October 1920 they had flown 462 operational missions, dropping 13,200 pounds of bombs. Three of them had lost their lives, and four others had been wounded. Behind them they left a lasting legacy of fighting spirit and tradition – and the badge of the 7th 'Kosciuszko' Squadron, which included the American stars and stripes.

The extent of the contribution made by this small band of volunteers to the Polish cause is summed up admirably in an excerpt from a report by the Polish Army Command on the Southern Front, written in the dark days when Budyonny's cavalry were still advancing on Warsaw.

> *Although very exhausted, the Americans are fighting as if possessed; without their help we would have broken down long ago.*

The Poles now had a period of time to rejoice in their new-found freedom. It would last for nineteen years.

CHAPTER THREE

Planning for Disaster: the Inter-War Years

The Second World War began on the shores of the Baltic Sea at dawn on the first day of September, 1939. Its origins had their genesis in the crippling terms imposed on Germany at the end of the Great War, two decades earlier; but it was the Munich Conference of September 1938, when the Prime Ministers of Britain and France agreed to the transfer of the German-speaking Czech territory of the Sudetenland to Germany, while guaranteeing the remaining frontiers of Czechoslovakia, that made Germany the dominant power in Europe and launched the cascade of events that led to the most terrible war in history.

Munich was the signal for the dictators of the world to do as they pleased, their paths illuminated by the arch-dictator of them all, Adolf Hitler. In October 1938 Germany occupied the Sudetenland and his ally, Benito Mussolini, declared that Libya was part of the Italian empire; and in November, Hungary annexed southern Slovakia.

The cascade gathered momentum in March 1939, when German troops occupied Bohemia and Moravia and declared that Slovakia was now a German protectorate. At the same time, Hungary annexed Ruthenia. Britain and France countered this wholesale dismemberment of Czechoslovakia with words of protest, and increased the pace of their rearmament.

The focus of European events now shifted briefly to Memel, the ancient Hanseatic port city lying on the Baltic at the mouth of the River Niemen. Part of the German Reich until 1918, with a population that was predominantly German, Memel had subsequently been placed under a French administration that governed under a League of Nations

'Peace in our time'. British Prime Minister Neville Chamberlain returns from Munich with the famous document bearing the signature of Adolf Hitler. The 'peace' lasted barely a year. (Author's collection)

mandate, and in 1924 it had been recognised as an autonomous region of Lithuania.

For the next decade and a half there was constant friction between the Germans of Memel and the Lithuanian administration, resulting in the imposition of martial law on two occasions, but the picture began to alter radically with the rise of National Socialism in the 1930s. In December 1938 the Nazis won 26 of the 29 seats on the city council, an event that led to the mass exodus of Memel's Jews.

In March 1939, the German Navy stood by to carry out a seaborne invasion of Memel. It was not necessary. The Lithuanian government gave in to Hitler's increasingly threatening demands, and on 21 March Memel was incorporated into the Third Reich. It was Hitler's last bloodless conquest.

On 28 March, Adolf Hitler repudiated a non-aggression pact, signed by Germany and Poland in 1934; three days later, Britain and France pledged their support for Poland if she should become the object of German aggression.

On 7 April, Italy invaded Albania as the first step in a planned conquest of Greece, an enterprise that would see Mussolini's armies meet with disaster. The disintegration of the League of Nations, which had vainly been trying to resolve the world's problems since 1920, was rapid now. Germany, Italy and Japan had already left the League, and now Hungary and Spain followed suit; the world's fascist dictatorships and military regimes were showing their contempt for the laws of humanity.

In May 1939, Denmark, Estonia and Latvia signed non-aggression pacts with Germany. With German influence and power in the Baltic growing, the Polish government was becoming increasingly nervous, particularly over the question of Danzig.

In 1919, under Articles 100 and 102 of the Treaty of Versailles, the port city of Danzig had been set up as a Free City under the protection of the League of Nations. Its harbour was administered by a mixed board of Poles and Danzigers under a neutral President, and the League of Nations was represented by a resident High Commissioner. Poland, meanwhile, continued to develop Gdynia as her principal port; this outlet to the Baltic lay at the head of the so-called Polish Corridor, the twenty-mile-wide strip of former German territory awarded to newly independent Poland by the Treaty of Versailles. Free German transit was permitted across the

Although of poor quality, this photograph clearly shows the despair written on the faces of German citizens, driven from their homes by the creation of the Polish Corridor through the territory of East Prussia. (Bundesachiv)

corridor, which separated East Prussia from the rest of Germany. Although the territory within the corridor had once formed part of Polish Pomerania, it contained a large German-speaking minority.

The existence of the Corridor was a source of growing and bitter friction between the Nazi regime and the Polish government, as was the status of Danzig, and in 1938 the German government began putting pressure on the Poles to reach an agreement that would see the return of that city to Germany. The Germans also wished to built a highway and a double-track railroad across the Polish corridor to connect Germany with Danzig and East Prussia. These proposals were rebuffed by the Polish ambassador in Berlin, Jozef Lipski, during a meeting with German Foreign Secretary Joachim von Ribbentropp, on 24 October 1938.

Five days later, Adolf Hitler issued a directive to the commanders in chief of the German armed forces. It ordered them to plan for the surprise occupation of Danzig by German troops. But this was only one aspect of the plan, for Hitler's ambition was the conquest of the whole of Poland.

Now, nearly a year later, as a foggy dawn broke on this first day of September, 1939, the plan was about to swing into action. Its objective was outlined by General von Brauchitsch, Commander-in-Chief of the German Army, in his first operational order for the campaign:

> *The object of the operation is the destruction of the Polish armed forces. The idea of execution is, by a surprise entry into the Polish territory, to forestall an orderly mobilisation and concentration of the Polish army and to destroy the mass of the Polish army expected west of the Vistula-Narew line by a concentric attack from Silesia on one side and from Pomerania-East Prussia on the other side. The expected interventions against this operation from Galicia must be forestalled.*

The key to the success of the campaign was surprise, in the form of a series of powerful attacks that would yield rapid results, and this envisaged the use of armour on an unprecedented scale. Two army groups – Army Group South, consisting of the Eighth, Tenth and Fourteenth Armies under Colonel-General Gerd von Rundstedt, and Army Group North, comprising the Third and Fourth Armies under Colonel-General Fedor von Bock – were formed to carry out the operation.

Attacking from Silesia, the main armoured force of Tenth Army was to thrust between Zawiercie and Wielun in the direction of Warsaw, secure the Vistula crossings and then, in conjunction with Army Group North, destroy enemy pockets of resistance in western Poland. Fourteenth Army was to cover the right flank of this attack with armoured support, while Eighth Army protected the left flank between

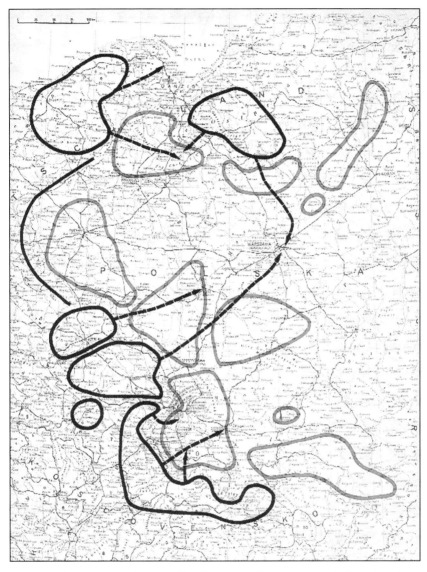

German strategic map showing the plan to break through, encircle and destroy the Polish armies in a lightning campaign.

Poznan and Kutno. Army Group North was to punch across the Polish Corridor and establish communications between Germany and East Prussia, then advance on Warsaw from East Prussia to cut off the enemy north of the Vistula. The *Luftwaffe* was to destroy the Polish Air Force, disrupt rail communications and support the army, while the *Kriegsmarine* was to keep open the sea routes to East Prussia and blockade the Gulf of Danzig.

Assembling the necessary forces was a stupendous task, made more difficult by Hitler's insistence that the mobilisation and advance to the frontier had to be undertaken in secrecy. To camouflage the massive movement of troops and equipment, eight infantry divisions were set to work, from June 1939 onwards, in building an 'East Wall' along certain sectors of the frontier, ostensibly for defensive purposes, behind which the German forces could assemble undetected. To strengthen the forces in East Prussia, certain units – including the IV Panzer Brigade – were openly transported by sea on the pretext of taking part in a big parade at the Tannenberg Memorial before participating in manoeuvres. The 'manoeuvres', when they came, would involve the full-scale invasion of Poland.

It was a bold and daring operational plan. The Tenth Army, commanded by General der Artillerie Walter von Reichenau, had to punch a 185-mile-long corridor through the enemy to Warsaw, using its armour as a massive battering-ram and ignoring its flanks and rear. Its principal task was to annihilate the Polish defences on the west bank of the Vistula before the Polish forces could withdraw to the opposite bank and set up a new line of resistance.

Simultaneous attacks, launched from the direction of Slovakia, Pomerania and East Prussia, had the object of containing the enemy forces and bridging the gap between the two army groups. The task of the III Army, advancing from East Prussia, was to exert pressure on the Polish forces on the eastern side of the Vistula, giving them no opportunity to manoeuvre.The main hazard foreseen by the German planners was that the Poles might decide to throw almost all their available forces against one of the two German army groups, leaving only a small force to fight a delaying action against the other.

The attack, originally, was scheduled to begin at 04.30 0n 26 August, and at 15.00 on the previous day Hitler confirmed that it was to proceed. Hitler was confident that all the loose ends were now tied up. Two days earlier, the German and Soviet foreign ministers had signed a non-aggression pact between Berlin and Moscow; it included a secret annex providing for the division of Poland between Germany and the Soviet Union.

Then came two political blows in quick succession. In the afternoon of 25 August, Hitler learned that the alliance between Britain and Poland, formalising the guarantee of 31 March, had been signed in London; and less than two hours later, Italian dictator Benito Mussolini, Hitler's ally, announced that Italy was not in a position to go to war on Germany's side. That evening, a visibly shaken Hitler withdrew the invasion order, and did not reinstate it until 31 August.

By that time, the mobilisation of the Polish armed forces had been officially announced. Europe was just hours away from war.

PART TWO

The Baltic War,
1939–1940

CHAPTER FOUR

Assault on the Baltic Coast

The bombardment by the *Schleswig-Holstein's* main armament of four 280mm and fourteen 150mm guns lasted for six minutes. In that time, the assault force, under cover of the fog and the smoke and the confusion, crossed the short distance to Westerplatte and stormed ashore, intent on overwhelming the outer screen of outposts at the edge of the forest.

Instead, the attack was met by heavy and accurate machine gun and rifle fire from three of the outposts. The marines, taking heavy losses, faltered and then broke. They regrouped and tried again, following a further bombardment by the *Schleswig-Holstein*, and once again they were repulsed with heavy losses. A third assault later in the day, this time supported by gunfire from the mainland and by troops of the SS *Danzig Heimwehr*, a militia force, and by combat engineers was also beaten off. At nightfall the defensive positions on Westerplatte still held out, although one of the outposts was destroyed and its commander, Lieutenant Leon Pajk, seriously wounded. The 75mm field gun, its crew having managed to fire 28 rounds at the German artillery on the mainland, was also knocked out by a salvo from the *Schleswig-Holstein*.

In Danzig itself, the SS *Heimwehr* quickly established control, although not without encountering fierce resistance, especially from a small group of Polish troops who had seized the main post office building. It took several hours before the Germans gained the upper hand, with the support of an armoured car.

On the first day of the invasion, while the gallant defenders of Westerplatte fought on, there was air and naval action in the Baltic as the *Luftwaffe* sought to render the Polish Navy ineffective. Bad visibility and generally poor weather conditions hampered air activity on 1 September, but Junkers Ju 87 Stuka dive-bombers of IV *Gruppe*, *Lehrgeschwader* 1

(IV/LG1) under *Hauptmann* Kogl sank the Polish torpedo boat *Mazur* in Oksywie harbour at about 1400.

In fact, Rear-Admiral Unrug, the Commander-in-Chief of the Polish Navy, conscious of its vulnerability under the threat of massive German air attack, and with the knowledge that seaborne operations would play very little part in the forthcoming invasion, had already ordered the main units of his fleet out of the danger zone. On 30 August, the destroyers *Blyskawica, Burza* and *Grom* had already sailed for Britain. One destroyer, the *Wicher*, remained, together with one minelayer, five submarines, two old torpedo boats, two gunboats, six small minesweepers and some auxiliary and training vessels.

On 2 September, Stukas of IV/LG1 sank the auxiliary vessels *Gdansk* and *Gdynia* (both 538 tons) in the Gulf of Danzig. Meanwhile, the battle for Westerplatte went on. It lasted for five more days, during which the defenders were subjected to repeated bombardments by naval gunfire and field heavy artillery, and attacks by dive-bombers. Much of the defence during this time was conducted by the second-in-command, Captain Franciszek Dabrowski, Major Sucharski having been in-capacitated by battle fatigue.

Early in the morning of 3 September, the Officer Commanding

Torpedo Boats, Rear-Admiral Gunter Lütjens, made a sortie towards the Hela peninsula in the Vistula delta with a force of destroyers. In an engagement with the Polish minelayer *Gryf*, the destroyer *Wicher* and a shore battery, the latter's 150mm shells obtained hits on the destroyer *Leberecht Maas*, killing four German sailors.

The Germans were soon to have their revenge. Later in the

The stern-faced Rear Admiral Gunter Lütjens commanded the German torpedo boat forces in the Baltic during the invasion of Poland. He was to lose his life on the battleship Bismarck. (Bundesarchiv) day, the destroyer *Wicher*, the minelayer *Gryf*, the gunboat *General Haller* and some smaller vessels were surprised at anchor off Hela by the Ju 87 Stukas of 4/Trägergruppe 186 (a unit formed for operation from the German aircraft carrier *Graf Zeppelin*, then under construction) and Heinkel He 115 floatplanes of Küstenfliegergruppen 506 and 706. All the Polish vessels were sunk.

Then came a new development. In the afternoon of 3 September, Admiral Lütjens was ordered to proceed with the destroyer force to Wilhelmshaven, from where the warships were to undertake minelaying operations in the North Sea. Germany was now at war with Britain and France. The move from the Baltic to the new operational area began early the next day.

The departure of the destroyers made it possible for the Polish Navy's submarines to operate with a greater degree of latitude. From its very beginnings in the early 1920s, the Polish Navy had made its submarine force the cornerstone of its defensive doctrine, and an approach to France in 1924 resulted, two years later, in the Polish government placing an order for three minelaying submarines of the Normand-Fenaux type. In Polish service the boats were designated the *Wilk* (Wolf) class, the *Wilk's* sister craft being the *Rys* (Lynx) and *Zbik* (Wildcat).

The *Wilk* class were large boats, displacing 980 tons surfaced and 1250 tons submerged, and were 250 feet long, carrying a crew of 54. They had six 21.5-inch torpedo tubes, one 3.9-inch deck gun and could carry 38 mines, but they were slow, making only fourteen knots on the surface and nine knots submerged. Basically enlarged versions of the French *Saphir* class, they were good seaworthy boats but had the major disadvantage of being noisy. Also, their external fuel tanks were prone to leakages and their minelaying system was unreliable. The first of the three was commissioned in 1932 and a Polish Submarine Division was formed under the command of Commodore Eugesiusz Plawski, the Polish officers and senior ratings being trained at the Ecole de Navigation Sous-Marin, Toulon.

As officers and ratings gained experience in the techniques of underwater warfare, it was decided to acquire two more large ocean-going submarines. The contract went to Holland, the first boat, the *Orzel* (Eagle) being built with the help of funds raised by public subscription. Launched on 15 January 1938 and commissioned on 2 February 1939, the *Orzel* was constructed at the De Schelde Navy Yard, Vlissingen (Flushing); her sister boat, *Sep* (Vulture) was built at the Rotterdam Dockyard. She was launched on 17 October 1938, but progress in completing her was slow, partly because of pro-German sympathies among the Dutch shipyard workers, and following the

The Polish submarine Sep *under construction at Rotterdam in 1938. She made a dramatic dash for home in 1939.* (National Museum, Warsaw)

German occupation of Czechoslovakia in March 1939 there were fears that she might be sabotaged. On 2 April, she put to sea for trials, but instead of returning to Rotterdam she sailed for the Baltic, still with some very surprised and indignant Dutch workers on board. With 100, miles still to go she ran out of fuel, and had to be towed into Gdynia, arriving on 18 April.

The two new boats were faster than their predecessors, having a speed on the surface of 19 knots. They were armed with eight 21-inch torpedo tubes, one 4-inch deck gun and one 40mm anti-aircraft gun; they were also equipped for mine warfare, with storage for 40 mines. They were 275 feet in length and had a displacement of 1092 tons surfaced and 1450 tons submerged. The deck gun was in a watertight compartment, allowing its crew to man it before the submarine surfaced.

On 24 August the Polish Navy's Commodore (Submarines),

Aleksander Mohuczy, placed all five boats on full combat readiness. Despite being the Polish Navy's main offensive weapon, the submarines were used defensively in the hours before the start of hostilities, adopting a defensive posture near Polish harbours; offensive plans were hamstrung by political considerations, the western Allies having asked the Poles to refrain from provocative acts.

During the first five days of hostilities the Polish submarines were frequently attacked by German aircraft and by U-boats, ten of which were operating in the Baltic. It was not until 4 September, following the declaration of war on Germany by Britain and France, that they were authorised to begin offensive operations.

On 4 and 5 September, while the *Schleswig-Holstein* and other warships continued to batter the Westerplatte defences, the *Rys, Wilk* and *Zbik* laid fifty mines north of the Vistula estuary, east of Hela and north-east of Heisternest. *Rys, Wilk* and a third submarine, *Sep*, were depth-charged and damaged by ships of the 1st Minesweeping Flotilla and most of the mines were soon cleared, although one claimed a German victim, the minesweeper M85, on 1 October, with the loss of 24 lives. Late on 5 September, all five boats were ordered to the northern Baltic to obtain some respite from the German attacks and to repair the damage they had sustained.

The problems facing the Polish submarines were numerous, and not the least of them was that they had no targets for their torpedoes. The Polish Admiralty had expected the Germans to carry out an amphibious landing on the Hela peninsula, but no such landing took place, so the submarines were redeployed on patrol duty in the central Baltic between the Danish island of Bornholm and the Gulf of Danzig from 8 September. They met with no success here, either.

On 7 September, the Westerplatte garrison, utterly exhausted, short of food, water and medical supplies, surrendered. For a week, two hundred and five Polish troops had beaten off attack after attack by a total of 2600 German soldiers, as well as withstanding a crippling bombardment. Astonishingly, Polish losses were only fourteen dead, with a further fifty-three wounded. German casualties amounted to some three hundred dead and wounded.

After the surrender, the Polish wireless operator, Sergeant Kazimierz Rasinski, was subjected to a brutal interrogation as his captors tried to obtain the secret Polish radio codes from him. He refused to divulge the information, so his interrogators took him away and shot him.

The ruins of Westerplatte's barracks and blockhouses are still there. One of the barracks has been turned into a museum, its entrance guarded by two shells from the *Schleswig-Holstein*.

German and Russian troops exchange pleasantries following the Soviet Union's invasion of eastern Poland. (Polish Ministry of Foreign Affairs)

Ironically, the gallant stand of the Westerplatte garrison deprived the Polish Navy of its one possible chance of success. At the outbreak of hostilities, the submarine *Orzel*, under Commander Kloczowski, stalked the *Schleswig-Holstein* for seven days, waiting for the battleship to emerge from the shallow waters of Danzig Bay and dodging several enemy attacks. On 8 September Kloczowski received orders to join the other submarines in interdicting enemy sea traffic, but on 9 September he suffered a nervous breakdown and took the submarine into the Estonian port of Tallinn in search of treatment, an action for which he was later court-martialled and cashiered.

On 11 September, with the Polish armies in a state of collapse and the Germans breaking through on all fronts, the Polish submarines were ordered to escape to Britain or, alternatively, to allow themselves to be interned in neutral Baltic ports. *Wilk* set out immediately, arriving at Rosyth on 20 September; *Sep* and *Rys*, which had sustained battle damage, sailed for Sweden with the undamaged *Zbik* and were interned there.

At Tallinn, following Kloczowski's departure for a hospital ashore, command of the *Orzel* was assumed by Lieutenant-Commander Jan Grudzinski. The pro-German Estonians informed the new captain that the submarine could not depart until 24 hours had elapsed, as a German merchant vessel had just sailed and this ruling was in accordance with international law.

At the end of the 24-hour period, armed Estonians boarded the *Orzel* and Grudzinski was told that the boat would be interned. The Estonians removed the breech mechanism of the deck gun, relieved the Poles of their small arms and started to unship the torpedoes. After fifteen torpedoes had been taken off the unloading process was sabotaged by *Orzel's* executive officer, Lieutenant Piasecki, who filed through the wire of the hoisting mechanism until it broke. The Estonians thought it was an accident and departed for the time being, whereupon Grudzinski began cutting the cables that held *Orzel* to the pier until only one remained intact. The guards on the submarine were completely oblivious as to what he was doing.

When night fell, the Estonians trained a searchlight on the submarine. At 02.00, acting on a prearranged signal, the *Orzel's* crew overpowered the Estonian guards, cut the last cable, started the engines and slipped away. Taken completely by surprise, the Estonians opened up with small arms fire, but the submarine was through the harbour entrance before heavier weapons fired on her, causing her to crash dive.

She spent the next few hours submerged and steering blindly, the Estonians having removed all her charts. From time to time the crew heard the screws of pursuing destroyers, but she evaded them successfully, and at dawn Grudzinski allowed her to settle on the bottom to await the next night. Numerous ships were heard during the daylight hours, and there was some random depth-charging, but the boat escaped damage.

She surfaced at midnight at the entrance to the Gulf of Finland, with no other vessels in sight. She still had five torpedoes left, so Grudzinski decided to hunt for enemy ships before departing for Britain. He was handicapped by the lack of charts, and several times the submarine collided with rocks, causing damage to the hull. On 22 September the Estonian guards were given a small inflatable dinghy, money, water, cigarettes and a bottle of whiskey, and were allowed to paddle to the Swedish island of Gotland. From Sweden they contacted their families with the news that they were safe and well, giving the lie to Estonian radio broadcasts claiming that they had been murdered by the Polish submariners.

The *Orzel* remained in the Baltic for over two weeks, surfacing at night in a vain attempt to locate German ships, but the only shipping seen was inside neutral waters. Finally, with supplies running low, Grudzinski decided it was time to head for Britain.

Escaping from the Baltic was far from easy. Grudzinski attempted to run through the narrows at periscope depth under cover of darkness, but the boat ran aground three times. With German destroyers patrolling in the vicinity, Grudzinski decided to take a risk. Blowing all ballast so that the submarine was riding high in the water, he proceeded through the narrows on the power of his electric motors alone, in order to minimise noise.

Undetected by the destroyers, *Orzel* reached deep water at last, but her problems were far from over. In the Kattegat, she encountered severe turbulence, so that Grudzinski had no choice but to start up the diesel engines. The sound attracted the attention of the German destroyers, but the boat lay on the bottom in silence for two hours until the patrol craft went away. Surfacing after dark, *Orzel* continued on her way until dawn, when Grudzinski took her down again until the following night.

She reached the British Isles on 14 October, 1939, having made radio contact during her passage across the North Sea. A British destroyer escorted her into harbour. As soon as he was ashore, Grudzinski made three requests. The first was to land a sick crew member, the second was to obtain replacement breech mechanisms for his guns, and the third was to receive orders for a war patrol.

It was not quite as simple as that; *Orzel* had to undergo some necessary modifications to conform with Royal Navy equipment requirements before she was fit for combat duty once more. She sailed on her first war patrol in British waters on 29 December, 1939, and operated with distinction during the Norwegian campaign in 1940, sinking two large enemy troop transports on 8 April. Lieutenant-Commander Grudzinski became the first of his countrymen to be awarded Poland's highest decoration for gallantry, the *Virtuti Militari*, in World War Two; he also received the British Distinguished Service Order.

On 23 May, 1940, during her seventh war patrol with the Royal Navy's 2nd Submarine Flotilla, she was lost with all hands, believed to have run into a newly-laid minefield.

CHAPTER FIVE

Winter War

The campaign in Poland was barely over when another bitter conflict flared up in the north. On 30 November, 1939, the Soviet Seventh, Eighth, Ninth and Fourteenth Armies launched a full-scale invasion along the whole length of the Soviet Union's frontier with Finland. The attack came after months of negotiations over territorial rights, in which the Russians claimed a large slice of Finnish territory, had broken down. As a pretext for this act of aggression, the Russians alleged that Finnish artillery had opened fire on a Soviet village.

The Soviet desire to acquire Finnish territory was all to do with defence, and in particular the defence of the city of Leningrad. After the western powers caved in to Hitler's demands at Munich, it seemed clear to the Soviet government that an attack on the USSR could be expected sooner rather than later. Russia began to look to her defences, and concluded that her most vulnerable city was Leningrad, which – situated as it was at the eastern end of the narrow Gulf of Finland – was wide open to attack by a naval power with command of the Baltic. Alternatively, or perhaps simultaneously, an enemy might attack by land through Finland, for the Russo-Finnish frontier was only twenty miles from Leningrad.

The Nazi-Soviet Pact of August 1939 bought time for the Russians to strengthen the defences around Leningrad. In addition, the acquisition of bases in Estonia and Latvia gave Russia command of the southern shore of the Gulf of Finland. With assurances of German goodwill following the signing of the Pact, the Soviet government felt confident that in the event of military action against Finland, Germany would not intervene.

What the Soviet government was offering Finland was an exchange of territory, but in the eyes of the Finns it was a poor deal. The USSR expected Finland to hand over parts of its territory that were considered crucial to Russia's defence; in return, Finland would acquire territory amounting to double the area, but in a non-vital part of the Russo-Finnish frontier. In brief, what this meant was that the frontier would be pushed back in the Karelian Isthmus area, making Leningrad more secure, while some islands in this area would also be handed over to the Russians to be fortified. Additionally, the Russians demanded a long-tern lease on the port of Hanko, situated in the south-west corner of Finland. With Hanko fortified, and a corresponding base on the southern shore in Estonia, Russia could command the entrance to the Gulf. Finally, Russia required territory near the Finnish port of Petsamo, so as to prevent an enemy from annexing the same area and threatening the sea route to Murmansk.

The Finns, with justification, could not agree to any of these requirements. For one thing, moving the frontier back in the isthmus would mean abandoning the best defensive line that the terrain offered, as well as a half-completed line of fortifications. To lease Hanko to the Russians was also out of the question, for with Hanko fortified by the Russians, Finland would be at the mercy of Moscow.

Several meetings in Moscow between the two sides, the last on 15 November 1939, resulted in stalemate. On the 29th, after Moscow had accused the Finnish army of shelling Russian territory, the USSR broke off diplomatic relations; and on the 30th, without warning, Soviet aircraft bombed the capital, Helsinki, and the Red Army advanced over the frontier.

In conjunction with the land assault, the Air Force of the Soviet Baltic Fleet attacked the island fortress of Russarö, commanding the approaches to Hanko, after which the island was subjected to a bombardment by the Soviet cruiser *Kirov* and two destroyers. At the same time, Soviet marines began landing on the islands lying in the inner Gulf of Finland, which were secured during the following week. Submarines of both sides were active from 3 December, the Russians sinking two merchant vessels (one German, the other Estonian). Finnish submarines attempted to attack the Soviet ice-breaker *Ermak* off Libau, Soviet shipping off Stockholm and warships bombarding Finnish shore positions, but met with no success.

The initial Soviet attacks were supported by four bomber brigades, some of them operating from bases in Estonia, and two fighter brigades – a total of around 900 aircraft. The bomber and reconnaissance units were equipped with Tupolev SB-2s and TB-3s, Ilyushin DB-3s, Polikarpov R-5s and R-Zs; the main equipment of the fighter unit was the Polikarpov I-15 and I-152, with only a small number of I-153s and I-16s. Because of their conviction that there would be no serious

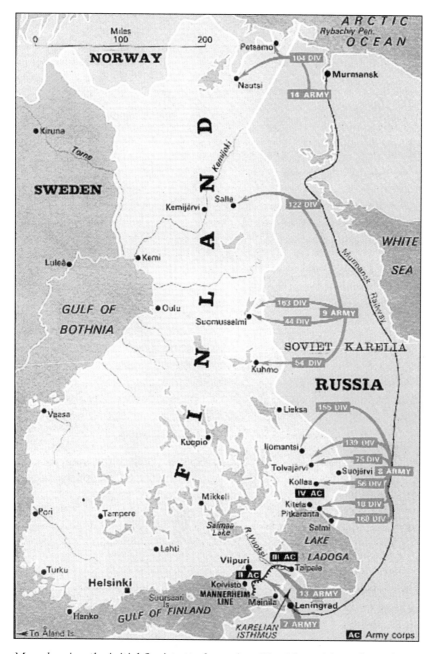

Map showing the initial Soviet attacks against Finnish positions along the frontier.

Soviet DB-3 (Il-4) bombers in formation. The DB-3 was the principal Russian long-range bomber.

opposition from the Finns, the Russians had not thought it necessary to commit their more modern fighter types to the battle.

The assumption that the Finnish Air Force would offer no dangerous resistance had been an easy one to make, for to oppose the formidable Russian air armada the Finns had only three air regiments with a total of 150 aircraft, mostly obsolescent types which included Fokker C.Xs and C.VEs, Blackburn Ripon floatplanes, Junkers K.43s and Bristol Bulldogs. The only Finnish aircraft that could really be classed as modern were sixteen Bristol Blenheim bombers and thirty-six Fokker D.XXI monoplane fighters.

On the first day of the war SB-2s and DB-3s attacked several targets in Finland, including Helsinki. Finnish fighters took off to intercept them, but all the bombers got away. On the following day, however, a pair of SB-2s was intercepted by Lieutenant Eino Luukkanen of the 24th Fighter Squadron, flying a Fokker D.XXI, and he shot down one of them. During the next two weeks, air operations were brought to a virtual standstill by heavy and continual falls of snow. Nevertheless, by 12 December the Soviet 7th Army, driving through the Karelian Isthmus, had succeeded in reaching the Mannerheim Line, the main Finnish defensive bastion, and the Russians were preparing to break through with their armour.

On 16 December the Russians threw in everything they had, con-

*The Finnish Air Force's most modern bomber type was the Bristol Blenheim.
This Blenheim Mk 1 previously served with No 601 Squadron RAF, and is
pictured just before delivery. The Finnish marking was a blue swastika on a
white disc.* (Author's collection)

centrating their main assault in the Summa sector. The attacking Red
Army units were preceded by waves of bombers – up to 200 aircraft in
all – which pounded the Finnish positions for several hours. Then the
Russian tanks went in, in groups of twenty-five or thirty. Scores of them
were halted by the Finnish anti-tank barrier and were picked off one by
one. Then the infantry attacked, the troops of the 123rd and 138th
Divisions moving forward through a ragged artillery barrage and
suffering terrible casualties. Fifty Soviet tanks managed to break through
to the town of Summa on the 19th, but they were mostly destroyed when
an attacking Finnish force cut them off from their supporting infantry.

In spite of the odds against them, the pilots of the Finnish Air Force
were very active during this phase of the fighting. Their orders were to
establish air superiority over the Summa area. By the 18th, Fokker D.XIIs
were maintaining standing patrols at squadron strength over the battle
area, and encounters with large Soviet air formations became more
frequent. The Finns usually managed to throw the Russians into confusion by diving through the middle of them, breaking up the enemy
formation and then concentrating on picking off individual Russian
aircraft. The tactics worked well, and several Finnish pilots began to
build up an impressive score of enemy aircraft destroyed.

In the far north, the Soviet Fourteenth Army succeeded in capturing

The main Soviet light tank used in the invasion of Finland was the T26, the Soviet version of the British Vickers six-ton tank. It suffered heavy losses. (Bundesarchiv)

the port and town of Petsamo and made some gains on the highway leading south-westward. At the centre of the front, however, the intended Soviet thrust across the narrowest part of Finland to the Gulf of Bothnia ended in disaster. The town of Suomussalmi was captured by the 44th and 163rd Divisions on 9 December, but they were driven out again the following day by crack Finnish ski troops and forced into full retreat. The Finns concentrated their attacks on the 44th Division as it straggled eastwards in temperatures as low as minus 40 degrees Fahrenheit, cutting off the Russians' line of retreat and sweeping down out of the forest to strike at isolated pockets of exhausted Red soldiers. By the end of the first week in January, the 44th Division had virtually ceased to exist. Because of the nature of the terrain and the almost wraith-like elusiveness of the Finnish units, the Soviet Air Force had been powerless to intervene.

It was a different story to the north of Lake Ladoga, where almost non-strop operations by Red Air Force units had saved a large part of the Soviet Eighth Army from what might have been complete annihilation. By the middle of December the Eighth Army had advanced thirty-five miles into Finland before being halted by deep snow and Finnish attacks. Then the Finnish 11th Division counter-attacked furiously, splitting up the Soviet 56th Corps into three groups which were then surrounded. The trapped Russians put up a fierce resistance and managed to hold on to their positions, thanks to daily supplies dropped by TB-3 aircraft.

As 1939 drew to a close the tempo of air fighting over Finland increased significantly. The Russians now realised that the tiny Finnish Air Force was proving a formidable opponent, and many of their bombing raids during late December were directed against Finnish airfields. They found it impossible to destroy the Finnish aircraft on the ground, however, for by this time the Finns had vacated their main bases and scattered their squadrons among a series of small and exceedingly well-camouflaged emergency airstrips. On Christmas Eve, for example, the 24th Fighter Squadron's pilots flew their Fokkers to Vuoksenlaakso, a frozen lake not far from the front line.

By the New Year, the 24th Squadron's score had risen to 100 Russian aircraft destroyed. On 3 January 1940 the squadron moved north-west to Utti, which was close to the Russian bombers' main route to targets in central Finland, and it was while flying from this base that Jorma Sarvanto, the 24th's leading pilot, achieved the most spectacular success of any Finnish pilot during the Winter War. On 6 January, 1940, Sarvato

Crack Finnish ski troops, seen here in action, inflicted disastrous losses on the Russian infantry, who had no winter camouflage smocks or proper winter clothing. (Ministry of Foreign Affairs, Finland)

was flying a lone patrol over the devastated town of Mikkeli when he sighted a formation of seven DB-3 bombers. Attacking through heavy defensive fire, he shot six of them down. The seventh only escaped because Sarvanto ran out of ammunition, but that too was shot down by other Finnish pilots as it crossed the front line.

On 11 January, 1940, a Swedish volunteer squadron joined the Finns in action. Known as *Flygflottijl* 19, it was equipped with twelve Gloster Gladiator and four Hawker Hart biplanes, operating from a frozen lake at Kemi under the command of Major Hugo Beckhammar. The Swedish squadron's first mission, a ground-attack sortie against Russian positions at Markajarvi, proved disastrous. Three Harts were shot down by ground fire and fighters, although one I-15 was destroyed by Ensign Jacoby, flying a Gladiator. A couple of days later, the squadron was dispersed among four small emergency landing strips code-named Svea, Nora, Oskar and Ulrik. On 17 January, four Gladiators led by Major Beckhammar encountered an equal number of I-15s over Salla; the Swedes shot down two of the Russians without loss to themselves. Early in February, an SB-2 bomber was shot down by Ensign Solvane over Oulu. Two weeks later, on the 21st, four Gladiators intercepted a Russian

A Russian Tupolev SB-2 bomber shot down by Finnish fighters. The Russians greatly underestimated the effectiveness of the small Finnish Air Force and the skill of its pilots. (Ministry of Foreign Affairs, Finland)

attack on Rovaniemi, and Ensign Steniger destroyed one SB-2 and possibly destroyed another. The Swedish unit remained in action until 10 March, when Ensign Karlsson closed the score by shooting down a big four-engined TB-3 bomber near Rovaniemi. During fifty-nine days of operations, the squadron had destroyed twelve enemy aircraft for the loss of three Gladiators and three Harts.

By the beginning of February 1940, the Russians had assembled a total of 1500 aircraft of all types on the Finnish front in preparation for the major offensive which, they hoped, would bring them victory. The I-15s were now supplemented by I-153s and I-16s, which began to appear in strength from the end of January, and a small number of I-17s, the latter for evaluation in combat.

The Soviet offensive began on 2 February, with a series of probing attacks all along the front and an intensive softening-up bombardment of the Mannerheim Line fortifications and the lines of communication to its rear by the Red Air Force. The main assault came at dawn on 12 February, with the Russian infantry advancing in the wake of a very accurate creeping barrage. The Russians had learned their lesson; they no longer attacked in densely-packed waves, but in small and mobile assault groups. The task of the Finnish defenders, already reeling under the hammer-blows of the Russian artillery, was made doubly difficult by blinding snow that swept across the terrain. As before, the Russians concentrated their heaviest attacks in the Summa sector, and on the 14th they succeeded in driving a wedge over two miles wide and three miles deep through the Finnish defences, forcing the Finns to fall back on their second line of fortifications.

Russian fighters roamed the sky of Finland freely now, outnumbering the defenders by ten to one. By this time, the Russians knew the location of every airstrip in Finland, and the Finnish air bases suffered heavily towards the end of February. Several of the Russian I-16 units became adept in hit-and-run intruder tactics, ranging deep inside Finnish territory in flights of three or four aircraft. On several occasions Finnish aircraft were caught by marauding I-16s just as they were landing or taking off, a number being lost in this way.

On 21 February, the worst blizzard in living memory screamed across Karelia, bringing both land and air operations to a halt for three days. The Russians made use of the respite to withdraw the exhausted shock troops of the Seventhth and Thirteenthth Armies, replacing them with fresh soldiers who launched a new offensive on the 28th. The Finns enjoyed no such respite; there were no reserves to relieve the battle-weary defenders of the Mannerheim Line. Nevertheless, for four days two undermanned Finnish divisions fought off twelve Soviet divisions and five tank brigades until they were finally driven back to the city of Viipuri, where – encircled and without hope – they made their last stand.

The main Soviet thrust against the city came across the ice-bound Bay of Virolahti, and suddenly the Finnish pilots got the opportunity they had been waiting for. The first Russian attempt to land a large force from the ice had been thrown into confusion by accurate artillery fire, and now every available aircraft was ordered into action against the disorganised masses of enemy troops And transport. The slaughter was frightful. Streams of bullets ricocheted across the ice, mowing down the enemy in swathes. The Russians broke and ran, trampling their wounded comrades into the bloodstained snow. They tried again, this time on the northern shore of Viipuri Bay. Soon the ice was littered with corpses, strewn among the carcases of burnt-out tanks and trucks.

For days the massacre went on as the Russians tried to smash through the last line of Finnish defence. Hundreds more Russians were drowned in freezing water when the Finns opened the locks of the Saimaa Canal, flooding the area around Viipuri. But it was the last act of the drama. The ten decimated Finnish divisions at the front, starved of reinforcements and ammunition, could no longer hold out. On 12 March 1940 an armistice was signed, and Soviet troops moved in to occupy the disputed territories.

The 'Winter War' had cost the Finns 22,849 men killed or missing in action, with a further 43,557 wounded, of whom 10,000 were permanently disabled. In addition, 826 civilians had been killed and 1538 injured in air raids. Soviet casualties remain unclear to this day. Russian estimates at the time placed the total of dead and wounded at 230,000, but other, more honest estimates raised this figure to 273,000 dead and 800,000 wounded, a truly staggering loss.

Towards the end of March, a fortnight or so after the armistice, the Soviet Defence Commissar, Marshal Voroshilov, presented a full report on the Finnish campaign to the Central Committee. It was hardly a shining chapter of Soviet military achievement. Apart from a few isolated cases, Red Army and Air Force commanders had shown a complete lack of initiative and tactical sense – a consequence, without doubt, of the Stalinist purges of 1937-38, which had robbed the Soviet armed forces of many of their best leaders.

Although over 150 major targets in Finland had been repeatedly bombed by the Red Air Force, the latter had completely failed to achieve its primary objective, which was to neutralise much of Finland's war industry. Because of the inefficiency of their navigation, formation flying and bombing accuracy, the Russians had persisted in attacking in broad daylight and under clear weather conditions right up to the last phase of the campaign, when some of their raids had taken place at night. Two hundred and eighty Russian aircraft had been shot down by Finnish fighters, and a further 314 had been destroyed by anti-aircraft fire. About 300 more aircraft of all types were written off during the four months of the campaign through accidents, mechanical defects resulting from the dreadful operating conditions, and battle damage, bringing the total losses to something in the order of 900. Against this staggering total, the Finns had lost only 62 aircraft in combat, although 69 more were so badly damaged that they could no longer operate.

The lack of success of the Soviet bombers over Finland had considerable influence on future Russian policy with regard to strategic bombing. The failure of the bombers to score any real success in the Finnish war, however, was without doubt a consequence of the very poor crew training standards rather than of any fault in the concept of this type of operation. Because of the ever-present fear of a surprise attack by the Germans, the Nazi-Soviet Pact notwithstanding, the best Air Force units were held in reserve in western Russia, and only began to make their appearance during the latter stages of the conflict with Finland. Towards the end of the campaign, the Russian bombers – which at the beginning had operated in formations of up to fifty or sixty – began to operate in units of twenty-five or thirty, under strong fighter escort. Bombers and fighters had been used extensively in support of ground operations, but their effectiveness had been drastically reduced by haphazard co-ordination and lack of cooperation between army and air force commanders.

The Finnish war had, however, been notable for one thing: the world's first large-scale use of airborne troops. On several occasions, commandos and saboteurs had been dropped behind the Finnish lines, and two airborne brigades had been used in action against the Mannerheim Line and during the Attacks on Petsamo. Although the Russians were later to develop the use of airborne troops to the point where they became an important and hard-hitting tactical weapon, these early operations were generally unsuccessful, the paratroops suffering from the same inaccuracy on the part of the Russian aircrews that saved many important Finnish target from their bombs. The airborne assaults lacked both planning and cohesion, the paratroops becoming widely scattered during the drops and consequently unable to attain their objectives. Several new airdrop techniques were carried out experimentally during the campaign, including the dropping of airborne troops without parachutes. The men jumped from low-flying TB-3s, relying on deep snowdrifts to break their fall. Surprisingly, the casualty figures incurred during these dramatic experiments were quite low, and most were the result of snow suffocation rather than impact injuries

The lessons of the Winter War were thoroughly evaluated by both sides. From Finland's point of view, the situation was grim. Her new frontier with the USSR was longer and much more open than the old one, and closer to vital centres of population and industry. In any future conflict with the Russians, the Finnish army would have to stand and fight on the frontier. This being the case, the key to military survival was modernisation. The Finnish command rose to the challenge, and by June 1941 Finland had a modern Army of sixteen divisions, with the benefit of modern equipment; the air force was also updated, receiving equipment from Britain, France and the USA.

The Russians, for their part, now appreciated the urgent need for flexible infantry tactics, better coordination between the different arms, proper preparation for winter warfare, and above all intensive and realistic battle training. The Red Army of June 1941 was a more effective fighting force as a result of what it had learned in Finland, but it terms of modern equipment it was still woefully deficient. It was also still deficient, as its soldiers would learn to their cost, in good leadership.

CHAPTER SIX

Training and Trials

lmost before the ink was dry on the Treaty of Versailles in 1919, and long before Adolf Hitler's Nazi Party came to power, Germany began a secret programme of rearmament. The German Navy had suffered particularly badly under the terms of the treaty, being forbidden to have a submarine service or to develop a naval air arm. In effect, the German Navy, its capital ships surrendered to the Allies (and most of them scuttled by their crews at Scapa Flow) was reduced to a coastal defence force, armed with a motley collection of obsolete warships which included eight old pre-war battleships, eight light cruisers, thirty-two destroyers and torpedo boats, some minesweepers, and auxiliary craft. If new capital ships were built in the future to replace the old vessels, their displacement was not to exceed 10,000 tons, while that of new-build cruisers was to be no greater than 6000 tons.

As German naval expansion continued, the Baltic Training Area – known simply as the Baltic Station, one of the German Navy's top three commands – assumed increasing importance. In 1924 its commander was Admiral Erich Raeder, who had left the Training Department in Berlin to take it over. Raeder had served as a staff officer to Admiral Franz von Hipper towards the end of the 1914-18 war, and had later been assigned the task of writing two volumes of the official German history of the war at sea, a work he completed whilst lying low in the Naval Historical Library, following an accusation that he had been involved in a Navy-backed uprising against the Weimar Government in 1920. These volumes dealt with the activities of German commerce raiders in distant waters during the war, and it was only while compiling this account that Raeder had become fully aware of the damage these vessels had inflicted on Allied shipping in every ocean. Not only that: they had also tied down large numbers of Allied capital ships and cruisers, diverted to search for them.

Admiral Erich Raeder was the architect of post-war German naval expansion. (Bundesarchiv)

In 1928 Admiral Raeder was appointed Chief of Naval Staff, just in time to steer the German Navy clear of a political storm. It was stirred up by the German Socialist Party (SPD), who discovered that plans were being laid to build a new class of warship. Known initially as *Panzerkreuzer* (armoured cruisers) and later as *Panzerschiffe* (armoured ships), they were designed from the start as commerce raiders, with a large and economical radius of action. In order to comply with the maximum tonnage specified by the various naval treaties of the 1920s, they were electrically welded to save weight and equipped with diesel engines. Their top speed of 26 knots made them fast enough to escape from any vessel that could not be overwhelmed by their main armament, which comprised six 11-inch guns.

Despite the SPD's vigorous campaign, conducted under the slogan 'Food not *Panzerkreuzer*', the building programme went ahead, not least because Raeder was an officer who was acceptable to all the German political parties. The first of the new ships, known as Schiff A or Ersatz *Preussen* (replacement for the old pre-dreadnought battleship *Preussen*, which had been placed on the reserve in 1922) was laid down by Deutsche Werke, Kiel, on 5 February 1929. The new warship displaced 11,700 tons and was officially named *Deutschland* at her launch on 19 May 1931. A second vessel in the class was laid down at Wilhemshaven as the Ersatz *Lothringen* (another pre-dreadnought, converted later to a minesweeper depot ship) on 25 June 1931, receiving the name *Admiral Scheer*, and a third, also laid down at Wilhelmshaven on 1 October 1932 as the Ersatz *Braunschweig* (the latter pre-dreadnought having been stricken in 1931) was named *Admiral Graf Spee* at her launch on 30 June 1934. There is little doubt that more of these fast, efficient 'pocket battleships' would have been ordered had not a change of naval policy followed the rise to power of Hitler and the National Socialist German Labour Party (NSDAP) in 1933

The relative seclusion of the Baltic was ideal for working-up these formidable new warships, and it was not until the Spanish Civil War, when they formed part of an international naval force blockading Spanish port, that the British and French had a chance to appraise them at close quarters. By this time – 1936 – the second phase of what was known as a *Shiffsbauersatzplan* (replacement shipbuilding programme) had already been implemented in Nazi Germany. It was secret, and it was under its umbrella that Adolf Hitler launched a major warship construction plan as part of his scheme to repudiate the Versailles Treaty and re-establish Germany as a world naval power.

The Nazis' rise to power had brought about a change in naval strategy. France was regarded as the main potential enemy of the future, rather than Britain, and a strategy for the conduct of naval warfare in the Atlantic, as well as the North Sea, was the main consideration. The immediate result was the construction of a new class of *Schlachtkreuzer* (Battlecruiser). Five ships were projected, but only two were started. The first of these, the 32,000-ton *Scharnhorst*, was laid down at Wilhelmshaven in April 1934; she was followed a year later by the *Gneisenau*.

The design of these powerful warships was based on that of the uncompleted Mackensen-class battlecruisers of 1914, which in turn were based on the *Derfflinger* of 1912 – arguably the best battlecruiser of its day. *Scharnhorst* was launched in October 1936 and *Gneisenau* in December the

The German armoured ship (pocket battleship) Deutschland *was the first of a new generation of German battleships. She was later renamed* Lützow. (Bundesarchiv)

The battlecruiser Scharnhorst *ploughing through heavy seas during a training exercise.* (US Navy)

same year. By this time, in May 1935, the *Reichsmarine* (Empire Navy) had been renamed the *Kriegsmarine* (War Navy), reflecting Hitler's determination to break free of the last shackles of the Treaty of Versailles.

In one area, and in conditions of strict secrecy, German naval experts had been operating in defiance of the Versailles Treaty for years before Hitler came to power. In 1922, operating from clandestine offices in the Netherlands and Spain, German submarine designers and constructors, under the guise of offering submersibles for service with foreign navies, began work on undersea craft which, in the fullness of time, would serve as prototypes for a new generation of German U-boats.

Some of the German-designed boats were built in Finland by Crichton-Vulcan at Aabo. Three of them, the *Vetehinen, Vesihiisi* and *Iku-Turso* (all named after water spirits in Finnish folklore) were laid down between September 1926 and early 1927 and completed in 1930-31; they were developed from the German UBIII type of the First World War and became the ancestors of the Type VII, which was to bear the brunt of the German U-boat offensive in the Second World War.

The other boat, *Vesikko* (Mink) was built at the secret request of the German Navy and launched in 1932, although she was not purchased by the Finnish government until 1936. The interim years were spent in cruising the Baltic and secretly training officers for the future German U-boat service. Great care was taken to preserve the true purpose of Submarine 707, as she was known throughout the Baltic, and a rumour was put about that she was destined for Estonia. A German officer, Commander Barttenburg, and an Engineer Assistant were appointed to the Finnish Naval Staff, and a German crew arrived in the special service ship *Grille* to take '707' through her trials. With the exception of four engine room ratings, the entire complement comprised young and eager German officers, a fresh team arriving each springtime. In this way, twenty or so potential U-boat officers each year received six months training in sophisticated attack methods at the expense of the Finns, and with the rest of the world being apparently none the wiser. Based on another First World War Type, the UBII, *Vesikko* served as a prototype for the coastal Type II.

In the mid-1930s, a new class of *Schwerer Kreuzer* (heavy cruiser) was also laid down. There were five ships in all, named *Lützow, Seydlitz, Prinz Eugen, Blücher* and *Admiral Hipper*. The first-named, launched in July 1939, was sold in 1940 to the Soviet Navy, in whose service she was successively named *Petropavlovsk* and *Tallinn*. The others were all launched between 1937 and 1939.

In the late 1930s, German naval strategy still revolved around the possibility of a future conflict in the Atlantic against a powerful French fleet, and the Munich Crisis of 1938 led Hitler – who had a very detailed knowledge of naval technology – to believe that there was also now the prospect of a naval confrontation with Britain. To be assured of naval supremacy on the high seas he needed a fleet of super-powerful battle-ships, two of which had already been laid down in 1936. These were the *Bismarck* and *Tirpitz*, respectively laid down as Schiff F Ersatz *Hannover* and Schiff G Ersatz *Schleswig-Holstein*. Formidably armed, displacing 41,700 tons in the case of *Bismarck* and 42,900 tons in the case of *Tirpitz*, their complement would be 2400 officers and men. Six even larger (56,200-ton) battleships were planned, known simply by the letters H, J, K, L, M and N. Only H and J were laid down, in 1938, and these would be broken up on the stocks in the summer of 1940, at a time when Germany believed that she had won the war.

One obvious deficiency in Germany's naval planning at the time of Hitler's rise to power in 1933 was that it did not include an aircraft carrier. Plans for one were drawn up without any input from the *Luftwaffe*, which showed no enthusiasm for the project, and in December 1936 construction began of the 23,200-ton *Graf Zeppelin*. She was launched in December 1938, but never finished; after many delays, work was halted in 1940 when she was 85 per cent complete. But that was not quite the end of the Graf Zeppelin story, as we shall see later.

U-boat activity accounted for much of the training scene in the Baltic in the late 1930s. Germany had begun rebuilding submarines in 1935, after Hitler formally repudiated the Treaty of Versailles; the first new boats built in German yards were the Type IIA of 250 tons, based on the Finnish *Vesikko*. Six of these craft were built, and were used exclusively

Captain Karl Dönitz, seen here as an admiral during World War Two, commanded the German U-boat fleet. (IWM)

for training. By the summer of 1939 the *Kriegsmarine* had 57 submarines of all types, under the command of Captain Karl Dönitz, an officer who had spent an undistinguished career in U-boats during the 1914-18 war.

The training system evolved by Dönitz was strict and inflexible, requiring a U-boat crew to undergo nine months of training in the Baltic and to carry out sixty-six simulated attacks before it was considered operational. They had plenty of targets, for in 1939 the majority of the German Navy's surface units, from battleships down to torpedo boats, were constantly exercising in the Baltic, honing their skills for the conflict that was to come.

That conflict was already a year old when, on 15 September, 1940, the mighty German battleship *Bismarck* left Hamburg, passed along the Elbe and through the Kaiser Wilhelm Canal, the 61-mile waterway joining the North Sea and the Baltic. Two days later she anchored at Scheerhafen, Kiel, and remained there for ten days, aligning her batteries and embarking supplies, before proceeding to Gotenhafen (Gdynia) in the Bay of Danzig, which was to be her base while she conducted pre-liminary trials in the Baltic. During October and November she carried out numerous tasks connected with a warship's acceptance trials, adjusting compasses, testing degaussing gear, running machinery and speed trials, and working up to her top speed of thirty knots. On 5 December she left the Baltic to complete her outfitting, returning through the Kiel Canal on 7-8 December and reaching Hamburg on the following day. Back in the Blohm & Voss shipyard and moored to the equipping pier, the *Bismarck* underwent final adjustments and had her last items of equipment installed, including the optical rangefinders and the full range of anti-aircraft armament. The final touches were completed by the end of January 1941, and the *Bismarck* was ready to return to the Baltic for operational trials. She did not sail until 6 March, and in the meantime her sister ship, the *Tirpitz,* was commissioned on 25 February 1941.

On 8 March, the *Bismarck*, having again passed through the Kiel Canal, embarked supplies at Scheerhafen in the course of the following week, while striped, dark-grey and white 'zig-zag' camouflage paint was applied to her hull. Superimposed on a grey band of paint, applied across the breadth of the deck near the bow, was a large swastika, necessary as an aircraft recognition marking. She also embarked two Arado Ar 196 floatplanes.

Based once more on Gotenhafen, *Bismarck* began her final series of exercises in the Baltic on 18 March. While these were in progress, she was joined by the new 14,000-ton heavy cruiser *Prinz Eugen*, whose captain, Helmuth Brinkmann from Lübeck, had been a classmate of *Bismarck's* captain, Rhinelander Ernst Lindemann, at Naval College. The *Prinz Eugen* was a formidable warship in her own right.

On 2 April 1941, the German Naval Staff issued preparatory orders for the deployment of *Bismarck* and other surface units to the Atlantic. In the next new moon period at the end of the month the *Bismarck, Prinz Eugen* and the battlecruiser *Gneisenau*, which was then in the French Atlantic port of Brest together with her sister ship, the *Scharnhorst*, were to rendezvous in the Atlantic to launch a combined attack on Allied shipping.

The *Scharnhorst* would be unable to join them as yet because her boilers were being repaired, yet even without her, it was a formidable battle squadron that was making ready to put to sea. Had it done so in its entirety, the result might have been disastrous for Britain, for *Bismarck* was capable of engaging escorting warships single-handed while her two consorts attacked the merchant convoys themselves. The carnage would have been terrible, as the British were well aware, having already had a taste of the destruction that could be meted out by major German surface units.

It was on 22 January 1941 that the *Scharnhorst* and the *Gneisenau* had left Kiel and broken out into the North Sea, heading for the commerce routes of the North Atlantic. They were sighted in passage on the following day, and the British Home Fleet, commanded by Admiral Sir John Tovey, set out to intercept them south of Iceland. Patrolling cruisers sighted them as they tried to break through, but contact was broken and the German warships withdrew into the Arctic for replenishment. On the night of 3-4 February, they passed through the Denmark Strait undetected, their murderous spree in the Atlantic about to begin.

On 8 February, in the North Atlantic, they sighted the British convoy HX106 east of Newfoundland, but the Fleet Commander, Admiral Günther Lutjens, thought it prudent not to attack as the merchantmen were escorted by the battleship HMS *Ramillies*. On 22 February, however, still about 500nm east of Newfoundland, they fell upon a westbound convoy that had dispersed and sank five ships totalling 25,784 tons.

On Saturday 15 March 1941, the two warships were operating in the central North Atlantic when they encountered the scattered ships of another dispersed convoy. The result was a massacre. The *Gneisenau* sank seven freighters totalling 26,693 tons and captured three tankers of 20,139 tons, while the *Scharnhorst* sank six ships totalling 35,080 tons. The *Gneisenau* had a narrow escape; as she was picking up survivors from her last victim, she was surprised by the battleship HMS *Rodney*, whose captain, alerted by a distress call, had detached his ship from convoy XH114 and rushed to the scene. The *Gneisenau's* skipper, Captain Fein, making good use of his ship's superior speed and manoeuvrability, managed to avoid an engagement with his more heavily-armed opponent, and got away.

The battleship Bismarck *seen from the heavy cruiser* Prinz Eugen *during exercises in the Baltic, March1941.* (US Navy)

*RAF Bomber Command was ordered to divert much of its strategic air
offensive against Germany into attacking the* Scharnhorst *and* Gneisenau.
*Here, a Halifax bomber is seen over Brest, with a smokescreen beginning to
hide the two battlecruisers, adjacent to one another at top centre. (IWM)*

The British Admiralty immediately launched a major operation to trap
the German warships, sending the battleships HMS *Rodney* and *King
George V* north, to join a third battleship, HMS *Nelson*, a cruiser and two
destroyers in covering the Iceland passages. Meanwhile, Force H, with
the battlecruiser *Renown*, the aircraft carrier *Ark Royal*, the cruiser *Sheffield*
and some destroyers, set out from Gibraltar to cover the approaches to
the French Atlantic ports, and on 20 March a Swordfish reconnaissance
aircraft from the carrier sighted the tankers captured by the *Gneisenau*.
With Force H coming up fast, the prize crews were forced to scuttle two
of the vessels, but the third managed to evade the British warships and

reached the Gironde estuary. The two German battlecruisers were also sighted by a Swordfish later in the day, but the aircraft had radio trouble and by the time its sighting report was transmitted the warships had slipped away. On 22 March they were met by the torpedo boats *Iltis* and *Jaguar* and some minesweepers and escorted into Brest. Their sortie had cost the Allies twenty-two ships totalling 115,622 tons.

Photographic reconnaissance by RAF Spitfires did not detect the presence of the German warships at Brest until 28 March, and as soon as he learned of it Prime Minister Winston Churchill issued a directive that the battlecruisers were to become a primary target for RAF Bomber Command. The air offensive against them began on the night of 30–31 March, when 109 aircraft were despatched to attack Brest Harbour without result. There was a further abortive attack on 4-5 April by 54 aircraft; their bombs caused considerable damage to the town and one fell in the dry dock alongside the *Gneisenau* without exploding. Her captain thought it advisable to move the ship to the outer harbour, where she would be safer if the bomb detonated while it was being disarmed.

She was located there by a photo-reconnaissance Spitfire, and a strike by Coastal Command aircraft was arranged. The sortie was flown at dawn on 6 April 1941 by six Bristol Beaufort torpedo-bombers of No 22 Squadron from St Eval, Cornwall, but only one succeeded in locating the target in bad visibility. Its pilot, Flying Officer Kenneth Campbell, made his torpedo run at mast height through intense flak put up by more than 250 guns around the anchorage, as well as three flak ships and the *Gneisenau's* own armament. The Beaufort was shot down with the loss of all its crew, but not before Campbell had released his torpedo at a range of 500 yards. The torpedo exploded on the *Gneisenau's* stern below the waterline, putting the battlecruiser out of action for months. For his gallant action, Campbell was posthumously awarded the Victoria Cross. The other members of his crew were Sergeants J.P. Scott, W. Mullis and R.W. Hillman. It was one of the bravest, and in retrospect, the most important, deeds of the war.

The Commander-in-Chief of the German Navy, Admiral Raeder, was now faced with a dilemma. He could postpone the planned Atlantic sortie until the *Bismarck's* sister ship, the *Tirpitz*, was ready to join her, but she was only just about to begin her trials, and the longer the mission was delayed, the less chance there would be of the ships breaking out into the Atlantic undetected, for the northern nights would soon be short. On the other hand, an immediate sortie would divert the Royal Navy's attention from the Mediterranean, where German forces had just invaded Greece.

On 8 April 1941, Fleet Commander Admiral Günther Lütjens, fresh from his Atlantic raiding experiences with the battlecruisers, flew to Paris to confer with Admiral Karl Dönitz about co-operation between *Bismarck* and U-boats. Then, on 24 April, came a further setback; the *Prinz Eugen* was damaged by a magnetic mine, and a fortnight was needed to make repairs. Once again, Raeder was forced to consider postponement, but despite the fact that Lütjens was in favour of it – at least until the *Scharnhorst* or *Tirpitz* was ready for deployment – he decided to go ahead with the sortie at the earliest opportunity. At the beginning of May, Lütjens flew to Gotenhafen and embarked on the *Bismarck* with the officers of his staff. The forthcoming operation was allocated a codename: *Rheinubung* (Rhine Exercise); the starting date was to be 18 May, 1941.

On 5 May, Adolf Hitler paid a visit to Gotenhafen, accompanied by, among others, General Keitel, Chief of the General Staff, and Captain von Puttkamer, Hitler's naval aide. Hitler spent four hours on board *Bismarck,* listening in fascination according to some accounts, to the technical explanations that were handed out to him. He then moved on to the *Tirpitz*, which had arrived at Gotenhafen for her trials. One of the men accompanying Hitler, Walther Hewel (Foreign Minister Joachim von Ribbentrop's liaison officer at Hitler's HQ), wrote in his diary that night: 'Visit unbelievably impressive. Concentration of force and the highest technical development.'

During the visit, Captain Topp, the *Tirpitz's* commander, who had been greatly encouraged by the success of the battleship's early trials, approached Hitler and begged permission to accompany the *Bismarck* on her Atlantic sortie. Hitler made no reply.

One of the men who waited on Hitler's entourage during their visit to the *Bismarck* was Captain Ernst Lindemann's steward, who had once been a waiter in Lindemann's favourite Hamburg restaurant. He had not liked the idea of military service, but had been happy to go to sea in a warship that was so large, powerful and safe.

As the day of the *Bismarck's* departure approached, the small fleet of escort vessels that would accompany her on the first leg of her voyage began to assemble. Foremost among them were three of Germany's latest destroyers: Z10 *Hans Lody*, Z16 *Friedrich Eckoldt*, and Z23. The 5th Minesweeping Flotilla would be responsible for clearing a path ahead of the warships, while three small flak ships guarded their flanks. Already at sea, in the Bismarck's operational area, were sixteen U-boats deployed to intercept any British warships, while a fleet of twenty tankers, supply vessels and weather ships were strung out along the warships' route, from the Arctic to mid-Atlantic.

On the morning of Sunday, 18 May, Admiral Lütjens held a final conference in his cabin, attended by his staff officers and the captains of the *Bismarck* and *Prinz Eugen*. His operational brief came from Admiral Carls of Naval Group Command North in Wilhelmshaven, who had authority over the sortie until the ships crossed the line between southern Greenland and the Hebrides, when it was to come under the control of Group Command West in Paris. Carls recommended sailing direct to Korsfjord near Bergen and remaining there for a day while the *Prinz Eugen*, whose radius of action was limited, replenished her tanks. The ships were then to sail direct for the Atlantic through the Iceland-Faeroes gap. Lütjens' intention, however, was to bypass Korsfjord and proceed directly to the Arctic Ocean, refuel from the tanker *Weissenburg* near Jan Mayen Island, and then make a high-speed dash for the Atlantic through the Denmark Straits. After the conference, Lütjens went over to the *Prinz Eugen* to carry out an inspection.

The two warships left harbour shortly after 1100 hours and dropped anchor in the Roads, and at 1130 the crews of both warships were told that *Rheinübung* was about to begin. In the afternoon, *Bismarck* and *Prinz Eugen* carried out exercises with the *Tirpitz*, the *Prinz Eugen* testing her degaussing equipment, and dropped anchor again in the Roads. The next few hours were spent in taking on fuel oil.

At about 0200 hours on Monday, 19 May 1941, both warships weighed anchor and proceeded westwards independently. At 1100 hours, they made rendezvous off Arkona, the northernmost cape of Prussia, and continued with their escort of minesweepers and destroyers. All that day, and through the night, the squadron sailed in formation westward and northward. Skirting the eastern edge of Kiel Bay, the ships passed through the Great Belt, the seaway that divides the two parts of Denmark, at about 0200 hours on Tuesday morning.

And so the *Bismarck* and *Prinz Eugen* sailed into history. Of the two, only the *Prinz Eugen* would return to the Baltic.

PART THREE

Barbarossa

CHAPTER SEVEN

Invasion

The orders issued by the German Army High Command (OKH) to Field Marshal Wilhelm von Leeb, commanding Army Group North, on 31 January, 1941, were quite specific. The Army Group was given the task

> . . . of destroying the enemy forces fighting in the Baltic theatre and, by the occupation of the Baltic ports and subsequently of Leningrad and Kronstadt, of depriving the Russian fleet of its bases. Timely co-operation with the strong and fast-moving forces of Army Group Centre will be ensured by OKH.

Leeb was well aware that his Army Group North faced the most daunting task of the three army groups earmarked for Operation Barbarossa, the invasion of the Soviet Union. Neither of the other two had such vast distances to cover, nor so little armour with which to make the attack. At his disposal Leeb had two infantry armies (Sixteenth Army under Colonel-General Busch, with eight infantry divisions, and Eighteenth Army under Colonel-General von Küchler, with seven); and IV Panzergruppe under Colonel-General Höppner with three Panzer divisions and five infantry divisions, of which two were motorised. Three more infantry divisions stood in reserve to back up Sixteenth Army.

The total strength of Army Group North therefore amounted to twenty infantry divisions, three Panzer divisions and three motorised infantry divisions, which compared less than favourably with Army Group Centre's forty-seven divisions. The enemy deployments facing the two army groups were also different. Whereas Field Marshal Fedor von Bock's Army Group Centre faced Soviet forces deployed on a wide but shallow front line, with a strong concentration in the Bialystok

salient which positively beckoned the Germans to encircle it, the
Russian deployment in the Baltic countries, recently occupied by Soviet
forces and now administered by pro-Soviet governments, was in much
greater depth. On the surface, it seemed impossible that Army Group
North would move fast enough to carry out a meaningful encircling
movement.

One factor, however, was in Leeb's favour. Although the USSR had
acquired a military presence in Latvia, Estonia and Lithuania following
the Nazi-Soviet Pact of August 1939, after threatening the three countries
with invasion, it was not until June 1940 that the Red Army deployed
there in strength, and a year later it was still unprepared to withstand a
surprise attack. Leeb therefore decided to leave the assault on the Baltic

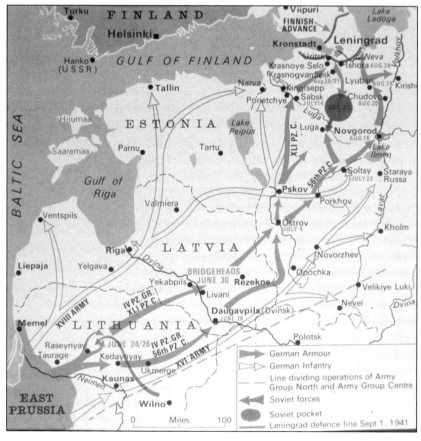

The German drive through the Baltic States to the gates of Leningrad.

States to Colonel-General Georg von Küchler's Eighteenth Army, while concentrating the Panzer units in the centre of his front. These would drive hard and fast towards Leningrad via Daugavpils (Dvinsk) and Pskov, their right flank protected by Sixteenth Army's motorised infantry divisions. Von Leeb's Army Group Order of 5 May, 1941, to IV Panzergruppe summed up the armour's task very clearly:

> *IV Panzergruppe will create the preliminary conditions for a wide and rapid thrust towards Leningrad. To reach the final objective, it is essential to move forward at every opportunity, as far as time and place allow, and thus to give the opposition no time to create any new defensive positions deep in the operational areas.*

Army Group North's offensive was to be supported by Colonel-General Alfred Keller's *Luftlotte* 1, with its HQ at Nordkitten/Insterburg in East Prussia. Its main asset comprised 1 *Fliegerkorps* under General Helmuth Förster, who had only recently assumed command; its operational air units were *Kampfgeschwader* 1, 76 and 77, all equipped with Junkers Ju 88 dive-bombers, and *Jagdgeschwader* 54, with Messerschmitt Bf 109 fighters.

The maritime air units earmarked for the operation were grouped within *Fliegerführer* Baltic under General Wild; this comprised *Küstenfliegergruppe* 806 with Ju 88s and *Aufklrärungsgruppe* 125 with a mixture of short-range reconnaissance floatplanes (Arado Ar 95s, Heinkel He 60s and He 114s).

German intelligence on the Soviet forces opposing Army Group North's advance was excellent. Since February 1941, German reconnaissance aircraft – Junkers Ju 88s and 86Ps, Heinkel He 111s and Dornier

Luftflotte *1's principal bomber asset at the time of Army Group North's attack was the excellent Junkers Ju 88.* (Bundesarchiv)

215s, all with specially modified engines to increase their operational ceiling, had been systematically photographing military airfields and installations all over the western part of the Soviet Union, operating at altitudes of between 30,000 and 39,000 feet. Undetected by the Russians, these overflights and many other sources had enabled the German High Command to build up a comprehensive picture of the Soviet forces in the path of all three Army groups.

Three Soviet Armies, the Eighth, Eleventh and Twenty-Seventh, were concentrated on the Soviet North-western Front. The latter was the weakest, with four infantry divisions positioned between Lake Pskov and Ulbena, in Estonia; the other two each had five infantry, two armoured and one mechanised infantry divisions. Eighth Army was responsible for defending the coastal area from Riga to the River Niemen as far as Kaunas, while Eleventh Army's defensive line ran along the Niemen to a point just north of Grodno. (See Appendix for the complete Soviet North-western Front Order of Battle)

Of the aviation assets available to the North-western Front, some 700 were fighters, but about half these were Polikarpov I-153 biplanes, with 160 of the more modern I-16s and about 100 MiG-3s. In contrast, the Soviet Air Force could provide about 400 bombers, most of them modern Tupolev SB-2s.

Daugavpils, with its twin bridges spanning the river Dvina, was an early objective in the German attack plan, and its capture was assigned to 56th Panzer Corps, on the right flank. XLI Panzer Corps, on the left, was to drive through Lithuania and push on across the border with Latvia to secure further bridgeheads on the Dvina between Yekabpils and Livani.

Operation Barbarossa, the invasion of the Soviet Union, was launched at 0305 hours in the morning of Sunday, 22 June 1941. At the apex of Army Group North's thrust, IV *Panzergruppe* crossed the East Prussian frontier and plunged on through Lithuania territory, encountering some active resistance near Taurage. This was quickly overcome, and by the evening of the first day the armoured spearhead had advanced thirty-seven miles in an easterly direction. There was as yet no sign of serious enemy resistance, but air reconnaissance had revealed strong columns of armour and motorised infantry moving from an area north-west of Vilno towards an important road junction at Kedaynyay.

This objective had been assigned to VIII Panzer Division, the spearhead of 56th Panzer Corps. Reconnaissance had reported that up to 350 Russian tanks were on the move, so it seemed that an engagement with VIII Panzer Division was inevitable. In the event, VIII Panzer made no contact with the Russians, who had passed through Kedaynyay and continued north-west, where they had been engaged by VI Panzer Division of XLI Panzer Corps at Raseynyay that afternoon.

The advance into the Baltic States provided a mixture of experiences for both the German troops and the civilian population. As one German soldier recalled:

> *Shortly before sunset we heard the soft melody of a lute coming from the bower adjoining the house. Lammerding and I found an old Lithuanian seated near the house playing to a few soldiers. His long, snow-white beard made him look like an ancient bard. We asked him into the house to play for us. He sat by the fireplace, his hands quivering over his instrument. Officers and men stood about or leaned against the walls and doorway listening in silence.*
>
> *As if out of distance depths that we could not at first comprehend came weird chords, first searching and then appealing, then gradually developing into a coherent theme of exquisite melody, sad, almost melancholic, yet with no touch of morbidness. To me these plaintive melodies were the expression of the soul of a frontier nation, which had suffered subjection and bondage for many centuries.*
>
> *Some of the soldiers who had been listening to the old man took the opportunity to have a look at the inside of the farmhouse. The massive stone oven in the centre of the living-room amused them; it was about twenty feet square, had an open fireplace and a number of apertures in which stood primitive-looking pots. The thick walls of the oven divided the house into semi-enclosed rooms.*
>
> *'Hey, Uncle!' called one of the soldiers. 'You must have a big family. Why do you want an oven as big as this?'*
>
> *The old man smiled; he knew enough German to understand what they were getting at. 'Will you be in Russia this winter?' he asked in his thin voice.*
>
> *'Perhaps.'*
>
> *'Then you will find out. And perhaps you won't laugh.'*
>
> *The prophetic nature of the remark then, at the height of summer, was probably lost on the German troops.*

As Army Group North continued its assault, a naval war was developing in the Baltic. It had begun on the night of 18/19 June, when the German minelayers *Preussen, Grille, Skaggerak* and *Versailles*, together with six boats of the 6th Minesweeping Flotilla under the command of Captain Bentlage, the Officer Commanding Minelayers, began laying a series of mine barrages between Memel and Öland in an operation lasting three nights. The Russian cruiser *Kirov* was sighted west of Libau in the

During their initial drive into the Baltic States, German troops were greeted as liberators.
(Bundesarchiv)

evening of 18 June, but made no move to interfere. Further minelaying operations were carried out on the night of 21/22 June by the minelayers *Tannenberg, Brummer* and *Hansestadt Danzig*, escorted by MTBs. The German force was attacked by two Soviet aircraft, but no damage was caused; enemy warships – destroyers this time – were again sighted, but kept well clear.

On the night of 22/23 June the Ju 88s of KFl.Gr. 806 joined the action, dropping 27 air mines on the approaches to Kronstadt naval base and attacking several vessels. Two steamers were sunk, one by a mine and the other by air attack.

Minelaying was also undertaken by the Finns, who had joined the Germans as co-belligerents. In their case, submarines were used. Soviet minelaying operations began on the night of 22/23 June, when various minelaying craft sowed barrages at the western exit of the Gulf of Finland, screened by cruisers and destroyers. One of the latter, the *Gnevny,* had her bow torn off by a German mine and sank, while another, the *Gordy*, was damaged by mines detonating in her bow paravanes. The cruiser *Maksim Gorki* also had her bow seriously damaged by a mine, but the destroyer *Steregushchi*, herself damaged, succeeded in towing the disabled warship to Tallinn.

Returning to the ground offensive, on 23 June the commander of IV Panzergruppe ordered 56th Panzer Corps to continue its thrust, while XLI Panzer Corps was ordered to complete the destruction of the Russian armoured force that had pushed on to Raseynyay. This proved to be the Soviet 2nd Armoured Division, and on 24–26 June it was surrounded and completely annihilated, not one of its 200 armoured fighting vehicles escaping. It was a one-sided contest; the Russian T26s, T28s and BTs were inferior to the German Panzer IIIs and IVs in every respect, and many Russian tanks were knocked out in the initial rush without having fired a shot. The key to the German success was, as it had been in Poland and France, excellent radio control, while the Russian control was either erratic or non-existent.

One type of Soviet tank, admittedly, was more than capable of holding its own against the Panzers, but it was committed only in small numbers. This was the KV-1, which, at the time of its appearance in 1941, was the most formidable tank in the world. Weighing just over 43 tons, and armed with one 76mm gun and three machine guns, it had a reliable 550hp diesel engine that gave it a range of over 200 miles. In Army Group North, 1 Panzer Division met it three days after the invasion. The division's own account tells the story:

Our companies opened fire at about 800 yards but it was ineffective. We moved closer and closer to the enemy, who for his part continued to approach us unconcerned. Very soon were facing each other at 50 to 100 metres. A fantastic exchange of fire took place without any visible German success. The Russian tanks continued to advance and all armour-piercing

The German Panzer III was superior to all other Soviet tanks except the Klim-Voroshilov (KV-1), which was too heavy to be really effective.
(Source unknown)

shells simply bounced off them. Thus we were soon faced with the alarming situation of the Russian tanks driving through the tanks of 1st Panzer Regiment towards our own infantry and rear areas. Our Panzer regiment therefore about-turned and drove back with the KV-1s, roughly in line with them. In the course of that operation we succeeded in immobilising some of them with special purpose shells at very close range.

The destruction of this mass of Soviet armour left the way clear for VII Panzer Division of 56th Panzer Corps, on the right, to push on relatively unhindered to Daugavpils, hard on the heels of a disorganised Russian rearguard, and in the early morning of 26 June a battle group fought its way into the town against stiffening resistance and captured the two bridges spanning the river Dvina. During the morning the Russians counter-attacked furiously, but their assaults were broken by the tanks of VIII Panzer Division, which came up to relieve VII Panzer, and by nightfall the Russians had been driven from the town.

Elsewhere Soviet resistance along the Dvina was feeble, and General Höppner ordered XLI Panzer Corps to attack on a broad front across the river below Daugavpils. On 30 June, bridgeheads were established near Livani and Yekabpils, and these were quickly exploited to form a wide bridgehead eighteen miles deep. The two Panzer corps replenished with remarkable speed, and by the morning of 2 July IV Panzergruppe was ready to proceed to its next objective, the Ostrov/Pskov area, the capture of which would open the way to Leningrad.

Throughout this first phase of the offensive, Army Group North had been effectively supported by the Junkers 88 dive-bombers of *Luftflotte* 1, with the Messerschmitt 109s of the JG 54 'Green Hearts' *Jagdgeschwader* providing cover. There was, however, remarkably little interference from the Soviet Air Force, and the official history of the Soviet Air Force in World War II, for a document published by the Defence Ministry of the former USSR, is remarkably candid about its shortcomings.

Units of the North-western Front Air Force (Commanding General L.P. Ionov) on the night of June 21 were carrying out training flights. In the morning when the flights had been completed and the support team was engaged in inspection and servicing their equipment, German bombers appeared in the sky. In spite of the suddenness of the attack, the enemy did not succeed in causing real losses either at the airfields or in the air.

The Air Force initiated military operations at ten or eleven o'clock. Bombers and ground-attack bombers in groups of from ten to eighteen aircraft began to strike at enemy tank columns near Tilsit, Taurage and

Palukne, and at crossings on the Niemen river. Fighters began battle with Fascist bombers. During the war's first day, the air force on this front flew more than 2000 sorties. In air battles Soviet fliers destroyed more than twenty enemy aircraft.

Despite the stubborn and heroic resistance of the Soviet armies and air forces, the enemy's tank and motorised divisions on the war's first day succeeded in penetrating 20 to 50 kilometres into Soviet territory. Many airfields were in danger of capture. Our air forces found it necessary to shift to the east, to the Mitavia and Dvinsk regions in Latvia.

Struggling to restrain the enemy's advance, troops on the North-western Front, in accordance with a directive from the General Headquarters of the High Command (Stavka), on June 23–25 made a counter-attack toward Sauliai and Tilsit. Almost all the aircraft of the Front and the 1st Long-Range Bomber Corps were engaged in support of this counter-attack. The battle raged for three days in this area on the ground and in the air.

Soviet fliers destroyed German tanks and troops in the battle area, flew cover for the Eighth and Eleventh Armies and also for units of the 3rd and 12th Mechanised Corps, and bombed railroad lines, stations, and reserves moving toward the front. Our fliers flew more than 2100 sorties in fulfilling these assignments. But the efforts of the Soviet Air Force in this period were scattered over a wide front, not concentrated in specific directions, and the air force did not have firm communications with the ground forces. This resulted in an unsatisfactory operational effectiveness. In

The Soviet Air Force suffered terrible losses on the ground during the German attack. The victim here is a Polikarpov I-16 'Rata' fighter.
(Bundesarchiv)

addition, our fighters did not succeed in providing constant and reliable protection for our strike forces on the ground, who suffered serious losses from enemy bomber attacks.

After stubborn and bloody battles with the superior forces of the enemy, the troops on the front were forced to retreat to the north-east. Having seized the initiative, the enemy by July 10 had advanced towards Leningrad and Pskov as much as 500 kilometres. In the first eighteen days of the war, the air force on the North-western Front flew more than 8000 sorties, causing significant losses in men and equipment. But our air force took serious losses in violent battles.

The *Panzergruppe* had resumed its advance on 2 July, swinging north-westwards, on a broad front, and on 4 July its northernmost division, I Panzer, captured Ostrov. In the south, after heavy fighting, VI Panzer Division punched its way through strong Soviet fortifications – part of the so-called 'Stalin Line' – on either side of the Daugavpils/Ostrov road, about eighteen miles south of Ostrov. By the end of the day, the three fast armoured divisions of General Erich von Manstein's 56th Panzer Corps, farther south, had penetrated as far as the former Latvian/Russian frontier.

A Panzer Mk III advancing past burning Russian transport. (Bundesarchiv)

On 5 July, the Russians launched an extremely disorganised and un-coordinated armoured counter-attack at Ostrov, where it was smashed by I Panzer. The Russian remnants withdrew, exhausted, leaving 140 tanks knocked out on the battlefield. Any hope the Russians might have entertained of regrouping and launching further counter-attacks in this sector vanished with the arrival of the bulk of 56th Panzer Corps armour, which had been diverted towards Ostrov from Opochka when the tanks encountered unexpectedly boggy terrain.

Meanwhile, the rapid German advance had created conditions amounting to panic in the Latvian port of Libau, or Liepaja, to give it its Latvian name. On 22 June, the Russians had 35 submarines either at sea or ready (at least by their standards) for operations in the Baltic, and fifteen of them, belonging to the 1st Submarine Flotilla, were at Libau, together with a destroyer And a miscellany of smaller craft. As soon as the German attack became known several of the submarines were sent to sea, one of them, the M-78, being intercepted and sunk off Windau by the German U144 (Lt Cdr von Mittelstaedt). The U144 was one of five U-boats operating in the Baltic at this time, the others being the U140, U142, U145 and U149.

On 24 June the commander of the Soviet submarine S-3, which had been refitting at Libau, decided to make a break for it, and loading his boat with shipyard workers – so that 100 men were on board, including his crew – tried to make a night run on the surface for Ust-Dvinsk. Unfortunately for him the slow-moving submarine was sighted by the German patrol boats S-35 and S-60, which attacked with 20mm cannon and hand grenades. The submarine's captain dived, but S-60 dropped a depth charge just ahead of the boat, which sealed her fate. A few survivors were picked up.

Most of the vessels in Libau harbour were scuttled to prevent capture, the submarines already at sea being diverted to Dünamünde (Daugavgriva), near Riga. Libau was entered on 27 June by units of the German 291st Infantry Division and a Naval Assault Detachment, the town being occupied fully on the 29th.

On 7 July, the two Panzer Corps continued their advance towards Leningrad along two major roads – the only roads extending through vast tracts of forest and marsh. With the bulk of the infantry formations now crossing the Dvina, but still a long way behind, this placed the armour in a potentially dangerous situation, as Soviet resistance was showing signs of stiffening and the Panzers' flanks were unprotected. General Höppner, who had hoped to be able to maintain IV Panzergruppe's momentum and punch his way through the dis-organised Russian defences to the outskirts of Leningrad, was therefore

A German machine gunner in position behind his MG34. (Bundesarchiv)

faced with a dilemma. Either he could proceed with the advance on Leningrad from the south-east, via Novgorod, or he could abandon the original plan and come up with a safer alternative.

An alternative, in fact, was suggested by General Reinhardt, commanding XLI Panzer Corps. His idea was that the *Panzergruppe* should head north via the lower course of the River Luga, even though it would mean negotiating over 100 miles of sandy, marshy tracks through a wilderness of forest, in order to reach the more favourable tank terrain bordering the Gulf of Finland, and then launch the assault on Leningrad from that direction.

After some deliberation, Höppner ordered Reinhardt to test the feasibility of this plan with XLI Corps, and by the evening of 14 July the bulk of Reinhardt's tanks had pushed through weak Soviet resistance to establish two bridgeheads over the Luga near Sabsk and Porietchye. For XLI Corps' 269th Division, however, it was a different story; this unit had run into strong resistance some twenty-five miles south of the town of Luga, and was virtually pinned down.The advance of 56th Panzer Corps had also been held up in front of Soltsy, thirty miles west of Lake Ilmen.

Despite these setbacks, Höppner was determined to thrust on to Leningrad, now only sixty miles away, but his plans were disrupted by an unanticipated turn of events. During the first two weeks of July, Sixteenth Army, advancing on the right flank of Army Group North, had been ordered to divert some of its formations to assist the operations of Army group Centre in the Bialystock/Minsk pocket, so that by mid-July only two of its corps, X and XXVIII, were left in support of the north-eastward advance. Then, on 14 July, X Corps, which was nearest to the Panzergruppe in the area east of Ostrov, was suddenly switched to the south-east to assist XXVIII Corps in completing the encirclement of a

Russian army at Novorzhev. With IV *Panzergruppe* poised to renew its advance on Leningrad, the redeployment of X Corps could not have come at a worse moment, as it opened a large gap between the *Panzergruppe* and the rest of Sixteenth Army.

Still determined to pursue the advance on Leningrad with all speed, von Leeb called on the help of Eighteenth Army, which had been making good progress through Estonia towards Tallin. He accordingly ordered I Army Corps (XI and XXI Infantry Divisions) to move eastwards from its present location south of Pskov through Porkhov towards Lake Ilmen, while XXXVIII Army Corps (I and 58th Infantry Divisions) was ordered to advance along the eastern shore of Lake Peipus towards Narva. Both corps now came under the command of IV *Panzergruppe*.

On 22 July the town of Soltsy fell to units of I Army Corps and 56th Panzer, but the German troops were exhausted by a combination of fierce fighting and summer heat and their attempts to advance as far as Lake Ilmen were checked twelve miles short of their objective.

The Soviet Air Force was increasingly active during July, as the official history states.

> *At the beginning of July, two regiments of the 2nd Composite Air Division were transferred from the airfield at Staraya Russa for action on the North-western Front, where a very difficult situation had developed. Carrying out their assignments under difficult weather conditions and without fighter cover, the bombers of these regiments in four days completed more than 530 sorties, dropping 250 bombs and inflicting serious losses on the enemy forces. Somewhat later, two more air divisions (the 41st Composite and the 39th Fighter Divisions) of the Northern Front were transferred to the section of the front held by troops defending the border at the Velikaya River.*
>
> *In the period from July 10 to September 30, our air forces protected and supported ground troops in all defence operations carried out by the Red Army with the purpose of stopping the offensive of the enemy, wearing down and exhausting his offensive forces, and disrupting his plan for a blitzkrieg.*
>
> *In the north-west area the German troops of Army Group North, after passing the line of Pskov-Ostrov-Opochka-Idritsa, attempted to capture Leningrad with the aid of Finnish troops. The enemy had a fourfold superiority in guns and mortars, twofold in infantry, and one and half fold in tanks and aircraft. He had 1900 aircraft of which 1200 operated directly over Leningrad. Our aircraft from the Northern and Northwestern Fronts, the Baltic Fleet Air Force and the 7th Fighter Air Corps of Air Defence had 1300 mainly outdated aircraft.*

The defensive efforts of our troops on the approaches to Leningrad began on July 11. The enemy's tanks and motorised divisions with the support of their aircraft went on the offensive simultaneously in the directions of Luga, Novgorod, Olonets, and Petrozavodsk. But the most dangerous of all were the enemy troops moving on Luga and Novgorod, who were attempting to break through on the shortest road to Leningrad. Therefore, around 70 per cent of our air power was concentrated on the battle with the enemy in these areas.

Operating in squadrons and flights, bombers and fighters struck at the enemy columns on the on the roads, destroying the enemy crossings on the Luga River and tanks and troops on the battlefield. On July 11 and 12 alone, Soviet fliers put out of commission in the Luga area 15 tanks and 90 armoured vehicles, and destroyed two bridges.

Our aircraft in the Novgorod area were not less successful. From July 14 to 18 they actively supported the 11th Army of the North-western Front, which was counter-attacking in the area of Soltsy. To support the 11th Army, not only the Air Force of the North-western Front, but also the 1st Corps of the Long-range Bombers and the 2nd Composite Division of the Northern Front Air Force were involved – in all around 235 planes. By day and night, the enemy troops were subjected to attacks from Soviet aircraft which during the five days of battle made 1500 sorties over targets in the area of Soltsy. In close cooperation with the air force, our troops caused many losses to the 8th Panzer Division, throwing it back 40 kilometres. The threat of a German breakthrough to Novgorod was averted for the time being.

By the end of July, the enemy offensive on Leningrad had been stopped. In the twenty-two days of battle on the distant approaches to the city, our air force flew 16,567 sorties and caused the enemy not inconsiderable losses.

Hopes of a rapid thrust to Leningrad had now dwindled to the point where they were virtually non-existent, forcing von Leeb to revise his plan of attack. First of all, his forces badly needed to rest and regroup, so Friday, 8 August was set as the start date for the renewed offensive.

The revised attack plan envisaged a drive on Novgorod via the western shore of Lake Ilmen by I and XXVIII Army Corps, supported by an additional four and a half divisions drawn from Sixteenth Army. On the left of Sixteenth Army, IV *Panzergruppe* was to attack in two separate groups; 56th Panzer Corps was to advance on either side of the Luga-Leningrad road, while XLI Corps was to debouch from the cramped Luga bridgehead, some sixty miles to the north-west. The objective of both corps was Krasnogvardeisk, and it was calculated that the two-pronged thrust would result in the encirclement and annihilation of substantial Soviet forces.

The morning of 8 August dawned under a leaden sky from which heavy and persistent rain fell. Denied their promised air support by the weather, the German divisions stormed out of the Luga bridgeheads into withering and intense artillery fire and ferocious Russian counter-attacks. After a day of fighting the Germans were able to report some slight gains on the right flank. but none at all on the left, where two German divisions were repulsed with heavy losses.

It was only after four days of intense fighting that the German attack showed signs of success. Soviet resistance slackened, the counter-attacks became less frequent and at last the attackers were able to break through a belt of forest to reach the open ground beyond. The three fast divisions of XLI Panzer Corps (soon to be reinforced by VIII Panzer Division, which had been assigned to it by HQ Army Group North) now turned east towards Leningrad, while I Infantry Division, which had taken part on the breakout from the left-hand bridgehead, swung north-west in the direction of Narva to support XXVIII Army Corps, which was heavily engaged.

Even for those German soldiers who had fought in Poland and France, fighting the Russians often came as an uncanny and unnerving experience, and a grim foretaste of what lay ahead, as this account reveals.

> *In open formation we started traversing the wood. We did not have to wait long, for after covering barely three hundred yards we were fired on. Close to me, Lieutenant Schleiermacher shouted, "Get ready to charge!" As we ran forward I noticed large figures climbing out of their holes which had so far been hidden by the dense undergrowth. Flames shot from all our muzzles. Thus, less than ten minutes after falling in, we were in close combat with the Russians; it was the first time we had got so near to them. I wish to God I could describe what it was like. I felt as if I were enveloped in a great heat from head to foot; I heard myself shout and scream; I pointed my machine-pistol towards the enemy and felt it tremble under the bursts of fire. Then a huge man appeared in front of me; he appeared as suddenly as if he had grown out of the earth. I held the machine-pistol against his belly, I shouted at the top of my voice, and as miraculously as he had risen, the man fell down again.*

The same writer describes a Russian attack in the forest.

> *. . . At last I saw them. The first of the tall brown figures were visible between the tree trunks. Bending down, they darted forward, threw*

themselves on the ground, jumped up again. There weren't single men any longer, but whole packs who gave me the horrible feeling that a horde of gorillas was approaching. There was something evil and ghostlike in the approach of these leaping, shouting attackers.

Their battle-cry sounded strange and uncanny. One of them, a sort of cheer-leader, intoned the "Ourrah" in a high tenor voice, and then the others joined in the shouting, taking it up in a monotonous voice, repeating the sound at regular intervals.

There was now frantic shooting from our side, and the figures nearest to us started collapsing. None of the Ivans got any nearer than about twenty yards. Lieutenant Schleiermacher shot from a kneeling position, the muzzle of his machine-pistol circling from right to left and back again. I lay three paces behind him, saving my bullets for the moment when I might have to defend my lieutenant from these fellows. With a peace of mind quite out of keeping with the situation I surveyed the whole scene every now and again. It occurred to me that if any more Russians came, we would be done for.

The ourrah-cries became less frequent. The brown figures which were still standing up, lying or kneeling amongst the trees, or which were trying to close in, no longer shouted. I could see mounds of dead Russians. And then a single, solitary, strangely plaintive ourrah-cry broke through the wood. Our weapons answered here and there and then they too fell silent. I stared towards the front in amazement; the attack had been repulsed and we had survived it.

On 16 August General Höppner's Panzergruppe captured Novgorod, and established a bridgehead across the River Volkhov. As the bulk of

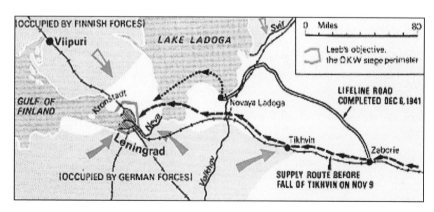

The isolation of Leningrad, 1941.

the Soviet forces had retreated eastwards across the river, the German advance was able to speed up again, and on 20 August Chudovo was captured. A week later, 56th Panzer Corps reached Lyuban, only fifty miles from Leningrad.

At this point, XXXIX Panzer Corps, detached from Army Group Centre on Hitler's direct order, joined the advance on Leningrad, approaching from the south-east. On 28 August, while its XVIII Motorised Infantry Division secured the Volkhov flank, XII Panzer Division advanced as far as Ishora, only eleven miles from the city centre. The XX Motorised Infantry Division, following it, turned north to the River Neva to secure the flank extending northwards to Lake Ladoga. The Panzer Corps was now in a dangerous position, its supply lines stretched to the limit, and exposed to Soviet counterattack from across the Volkhov.

XLI Panzer Corps, meanwhile, had reached the Krasnogvardiesk/ Krasnoye Selo line, where it too had been held up to await replenishment. On 21 August, all XLI Corps units still capable of fighting were ordered to regroup and move south under the leadership of VIII Panzer Division to attack the rear of the Soviet forces bypassed in the Luga area. These forces, deprived of supplies, were mopped up during the first fortnight of September, 20,000 prisoners being taken.

The fate of Leningrad now appeared sealed. The city was trapped between Army Group North, now occupying virtually all the coastline of the Gulf of Finland, and Marshal Mannerheim's Karelian Army, fighting its way through the forests around Lake Ladoga.

CHAPTER EIGHT

The Finnish Front

G iven the savage losses inflicted on the Finns by the Russians during the Winter War, there was never much doubt that Finland would side with Germany when the latter launched its assault on the USSR. Already, in August 1940, the Finnish Government had agreed to transit rights for German troops en route to and from Norway, and by the spring of 1941 the Germans had set up a substantial base system in northern Finland. From this jumping-off point they could, if necessary, secure the large nickel deposits in northern Finland, and when the time came, attack towards the vital north Russian port of Murmansk.

In May 1941 the Finnish Government tacitly agreed to participate in the planned German operations on the Northern Front. While German forces advanced on Murmansk, the bulk of the Finnish army would strike south into Soviet Karelia, threatening Leningrad from the north.

The German-Finnish offensive in the north was not scheduled to begin until 28 June, a week after the commencement of Operation Barbarossa. The Russians, however, quickly became aware of the extent of German activity in Finland, and on 25 June, in one of the few successful Russian air operations during the initial phase, 236 bombers of the Soviet 2nd, 41st, 55th and 5th (Composite) Air Divisions, escorted by 224 fighters, bombed nineteen airfields in northern Norway and Finland. The Russians claimed the destruction of forty-one enemy aircraft.

The offensive in the north was under the command of Colonel-General Nikolaus von Falkenhorst, commanding the German Army of Occupation in Norway. In the extreme north, on the shores of the Arctic Ocean and poised to strike at Murmansk, was General Eduard Dietl's Gebirgskorps (Mountain Corps), with two divisions. In the centre was XXXVI Army Corps, comprising the 169th Division, SS Panzer Division, and the Finnish VI Division, based on Rovaniemi, while the right flank

After the armistice of March 1940, Finland built a strongly-fortified defensive position known as the Mannerheim Line across the Karelian Isthmus.

was covered by the Finnish III Army Corps, consisting of a single division.

Beyond this, to the south of a demarcation line running through Oulu, were thirteen Finnish divisions and three brigades under the command of General Erik Heinrichs, the whole ensemble of four army corps known as the Army of Karelia. The bulk of this force faced south-east, confronting the Soviet Twenty-Third Army with four divisions under General Gerasimov, covering the direct approach to Leningrad from the north. The frontier from Lake Ladoga to Yhta, in the centre, was covered by General Meretskov's Seventh Army, with only three divisions plus two in reserve, while the northern sector, covering the approaches to Murmansk and the White Sea, was held by the Fourteenth Army, with four divisions and an armoured division in reserve. The Russians also held the fortress of Hanko on the Gulf of Finland, ceded under the armistice terms of 1940, with a garrison of 27,000 men.

In the north, a combination of difficult terrain and stiffening Russian resistance soon caused Falkenhorst's offensive to become bogged down. On the left flank, successive thrusts towards Murmansk were halted on the line of the River Litsa in September, forcing the Germans to dig in for the winter, while in the centre the attack was halted just short of Yhta, the first major objective.

The attack by Marshal Mannerheim's Karelian Army opened on 10 July. The Finns enjoyed a superiority of two to one and succeeded in breaking through the Russian frontier defences, pushing on rapidly to Lake Ladoga and cutting the Russian front in two. VI Army Corps now advanced south-eastwards through the wilderness that bordered Lake Ladoga, and on 1 September, on Mannerheim's orders, halted on a line running from Vidlitsa to a point south-west of Lake Segozero. In the south, the Finns trapped the Soviet 198th and 142nd Divisions against Lake Ladoga and drove on to the Vuoksi river, crossing over to form a bridgehead at Vuosalmi on 11 August. On the Gulf of Finland, the Russians in the Viipuri sector, their rear threatened by the Finnish advance on Vuoksi, began to withdraw, their movement assisted by two Soviet divisions which put pressure on the attacking Finns. Although this slowed the Finnish advance, by 27 August Mannerheim's forces had cut the main road and railway to Leningrad and were relentlessly

Finnish artillery in action. The gun is a 150mm howitzer of German origin.
(Source unknown)

squeezing three Russian divisions that were scrambling to escape through a gap just over four miles wide.

The destruction of these three divisions was avoided only because Marshal Mannerheim ordered his forces on the Vuoksi to make a rapid advance down the Karelian Isthmus and occupy the territory that had been Finland's prior to the Winter War. As a consequence, two of the Soviet divisions escaped, and a third took refuge on Koivisto island, from where most of the troops were later evacuated by sea.

The Germans were now putting intense pressure on Marshal Mannerheim to continue the offensive by pushing down behind Leningrad to link up with German forces on the Neva and then launching a full-scale assault on the city. Mannerheim refused, stating that the Finnish government had no desire to take part in an attack on Leningrad, and in any case his forces were in no position to do so, lacking the necessary dive-bombers and heavy artillery. It was a decision which, ultimately, was to be the salvation of Leningrad, for had the Germans and Finns launched a coordinated offensive against the city in September 1941 there is little doubt that its defences would have been overwhelmed and that it would have been cut off from its lifeline of Lake Ladoga.

As it was, the Finns contented themselves with completing the second phase of their offensive in Karelia. Their attack, which was completely successful, began on 3 September, their motorised troops pushing on through Olonets to the River Svir and cutting the Murmansk-Leningrad railway at Lodenoe Pole. On the left, the Finns attacked along the main railway line to Petrozavodsk, the capital of Soviet Karelia, and on 12 September they joined up with the force on the Svir to form a common front. Petrozavodsk eventually fell on 1 October, after bitter fighting.

As the first heavy autumn rains turned the summer dust into clinging mud, the *Luftwaffe* and the Finnish Air Force began to encounter new types of Soviet combat aircraft in growing numbers. Combat experience gained by the Soviet Air Force during the first three months of the war was already enabling Russian designers to incorporate a number of modifications in their new monoplane fighters. The MiG-1 was re-designated MiG-3 after the 2100th machine had been produced, the main improvements being a fully enclosed cockpit and the addition of an auxiliary fuel tank. Because of the increased combat radius that resulted, MiG-3s were used extensively for fast reconnaissance. The light and manoeuvrable little Yakovlev Yak-1, known to its pilots as 'Krasavyets' (Beauty), was also modified, being given a heavier armament and an improved engine.

The third fighter type, the LaGG-3, had proved a disappointment in combat with German fighters. Although its flight characteristics were

Finland's top-scoring air ace was Warrant Officer Ilmari Juutilainen, who destroyed 94 Russian aircraft in the 'Winter War' and 'Continuation War.' He is seen here with his Brewster Buffalo fighter.
(Author's collection)

excellent in level flight, acceleration was poor and the aircraft was sloppy during the tight manoeuvres necessary under combat conditions, with a marked tendency to spin out of tight turns. It was eventually discovered that this unpleasant habit could be cured completely by lowering ten or fifteen degrees of flap, which permitted a pilot to turn as tightly as he liked. In spite of its faults, the LaGG-3 enjoyed a better reputation with Soviet pilots than the MiG-3. Conceived as a high-altitude interceptor, the latter suffered a dramatic loss of performance when circumstances forced it to be adapted to other tasks.

On the Karelian Front, Soviet aircrews found themselves in action against a remarkable miscellany of Finnish aircraft, including captured Russian types like the Polikarpov I-153, which the Finns used for reconnaissance, and the SB-2 bomber, used for maritime reconnaissance. The Finnish fighter assets, as well as the Fokker D.XXI, now included Brewster Buffaloes, Fiat G.50s, Morane 406s, Gloster Gladiators and Hawker Hurricanes, while a modern bomber element comprised three squadrons of Bristol Blenheims. In total, the Finnish Air Force could field fourteen first-line squadrons.

Meanwhile, a strategic air war was developing to a limited extent on the Eastern Front. On the night of 21/22 July, Moscow was attacked for the first time by Ju 88s of KG 3 and KG 54 and Heinkel He 111s of KG 28, 53 and 55, with *Kampfgruppe* 100 and III/KG 26 forming a pathfinder force. The 127 bombers, flying over distances of up to 380 miles to the Russian capital, attacked through very heavy AA and searchlight defences, dropping 104 tons of high explosive and 46,000 incendiary bombs. The bombing was haphazard and generally ineffective. On the next night 115 bombers were despatched to Moscow, but after that the numbers declined. Of the 76 raids on Moscow in 1941, 59 were carried out by groups of between three and ten aircraft. The lack of a long-range strategic bombing force was to be a hindrance to the *Luftwaffe* during the campaign in Russia; the Soviet government quickly set up war production factories that were out of range of existing bomber aircraft.

The Soviet Air Force suffered from a similar deficiency, and its early attempts at strategic bombing were little more than pinpricks. Soon after the *Luftwaffe*'s first raids on Moscow, for example, the Soviet Air Force was ordered to retaliate by bombing Berlin. It was easier said than done. The only Russian bomber with sufficient range for the job was the Ilyushin Il-4 (DB-3F), and the only Il-4s that still occupied bases within striking distance of the German capital a month after the invasion were naval aircraft, operating with the Baltic Fleet from the Estonian islands of Dagö and Oesel. Two squadrons of these – a total of thirteen aircraft – were hurriedly formed into a makeshift bombing force under the leadership of an air force officer, Colonel E.N. Preobrazhenski, commander of the 1st Bomber Aviation Regiment of the Baltic Fleet, and on 7 August five Il-4s took off on the 1500-mile round trip. Two of the bombers were shot down during the outward flight, two more failed to find the target, and one bombed the suburbs of Berlin, causing insignificant damage. Four more raids were carried out between 7 August and 4 September, but few of the attacking aircraft managed to find the target and 75 per cent losses were sustained. Finally, in mid-September, the evacuation of the Russian bases in the face of the German thrust through Estonia brought an end to these operations.

In the Baltic, meanwhile, the Russians had been forced to evacuate Riga and Dünamünde on 30 June, their naval units – including the cruiser *Kirov* – making for Tallinn. Minelaying and minesweeping by both sides

Attacks on Berlin were also carried out by four-engined Petlyakov Pe-8 bombers, operating from a base near Leningrad, but very few were available for such missions. (Author's collection)

continued at an intense rate, several smaller German and Soviet vessels being lost during these operations. German MTBs carried out a number of daring attacks during this period, including one on a Soviet destroyer in the Bay of Riga on 15 July. These attacks were generally unsuccessful, but three days later a Ju 88 of K.Fl.Gr 806 severely damaged the destroyer *Serdity*, causing her to be abandoned and scuttled in Moon Sound. A few days later, the same unit also bombed and sank the destroyer *Karl Marks* in Loksa Bay, near Tallinn.

On 28 July, the Germans suffered their first submarine loss of the campaign when the U144 was torpedoed and sunk by the Soviet submarine Shch-307 (Lt Cdr Petrov) off the Gulf of Finland.

By the last week of August, it was apparent that the naval base at Tallinn could not be held, and arrangements were made to evacuate it. On the night of 27/28 August, units of the Soviet X Corps were embarked on several convoys, which then assembled in Tallinn Roads. The evacuation took place under heavy air attack by Ju 88s, the convoys having to make their way in darkness through a narrow channel that had been swept through the minefields. Of the 195 merchant vessels and escorting warships, 53 were lost en route. The Baltic Red Fleet lost five destroyers, two submarines, two corvettes and two smaller units in the minefields, while of the twenty-nine large merchant vessels that left Tallinn only one reached Kronstadt, twenty-five being sunk and three more beached. Of the thirty-eight smaller vessels that took part in the evacuation, nine were lost. In all, 18,000 men reached Leningrad, but 6000 were lost. For the Russians, it was a disaster on a huge scale, and there were more to follow.

CHAPTER NINE

The Ordeal of Leningrad

In late August 1941, two *Stukagruppen* – 1/St.G 2 and III/St.G 2 – which had been operating in support of Army Group Centre under the command of Major Oskar Dinort, were redeployed to the Leningrad Front for intensive operations against lines of communication between Moscow and Leningrad, coming under the orders of *Luftflotte* 1. The Stukas were based at Tyrkovo, some ninety miles west of Lake Ilmen.

The German offensive in this sector, faced with fierce resistance and increasingly poor weather, had now become bogged down, and operations had degenerated into a slogging match between the opposing sides' artillery. Much of the Russians' gunfire support was provided by the warships of the Baltic Fleet. One group, comprising three destroyers and three gunboats, was on the River Neva, supporting the Forty-Second and Fifty-Fifth Armies south-east of Leningrad; another group operated in the waters of the canal that linked Leningrad with the White Sea. This group included the cruiser *Maksim Gorki*, which had lost her bows to a mine on 23 June and had undergone temporary repairs; the cruiser *Petropavlovsk*; and six destroyers. The third and most powerful group

The Junkers Ju 87 Stuka dive-bomber was to play a vital part in immobilising the major units of the Soviet Baltic Fleet in Kronstadt.
(Author's collection)

The heavy guns of the battleship Marat *posed a considerable threat to the German Eighteenth Army, advancing on Leningrad.* (Baltic Zavod)

was in Kronstadt Bay, and comprised the battleships *Oktyabrskaya Revolutsiya* and *Marat*, the cruiser *Kirov*, the flotilla leader *Minsk* and six destroyers, two of which were under repair.

The two battleships were of major concern to the Germans. Both were old, having been completed in 1915, and both had been damaged by gunfire from German shore batteries. However, they were still seaworthy, and carried a formidable armament of twelve 12-inch and sixteen 4.7-inch guns, as well as six 76mm anti-aircraft guns and a host of smaller-calibre weapons. The troublesome nature of these warships was highlighted on 7 September, when *Maksim Gorki*, positioned in the Leningrad merchant harbour, and *Marat*, stationed in the White Sea Canal, fired on advance units of the German Eighteenth Army and brought them to a standstill. The following day, *Oktyabrskaya Revolutsiya, Kirov* and the gunboat *Krasnoya Znamya* joined forces in shelling German assembly areas near Oranienbaum, Krasnoye Selo and Peterhof. On 16 September, following a breakthough by German forces into Kronstadt Bay near Peterhof, German coastal batteries opened fire on *Marat* and *Petropavlovsk*; both were hit by 6-inch shells, which had hardly any effect on their thick armour. It was clear that the warships would have to be neutralised from the air, by precise dive-bombing attacks.

Beginning on 21 September, 1941, St.G 2 launched an all-out offensive. Attacking the warships was extremely dangerous, as explained by

St.G 2 dive-bomber ace Lieutenant Hans-Ulrich Rudel in his book *Stuka Pilot.*

After our first sortie our luck with the weather is out. Always a brilliant blue sky and murderous flak. I never again experience anything to compare with it in any place or theatre of war. Our reconnaissance estimates that a hundred AA guns are concentrated in an area of six square miles in the target zone. The flak bursts form a whole cumulus of cloud. If the explosions are more than 10 or 12 feet away one cannot hear the flak from the flying aircraft. But we hear no single bursts; rather an incessant tempest of noise like the clap of doomsday. The concentrated zones of flak in the air space begin as soon as we cross the coastal strip which is still in Soviet hands. Then come Oranienbaum and Peterhof; being harbours, very strongly defended. The open water is alive with pontoons, barges, boats and tiny craft, all stiff with flak. The Russians use every possible site for their AA guns. For instance, the mouth of Leningrad harbour is supposed to have been closed to our U-boats by means of huge steel nets suspended from a chain of concrete blocks floating on the surface of the water. Even from these blocks AA guns bark at us.

After about another six miles we sight the island of Kronstadt with its great naval harbour and the town of the same name. Both harbour and town are heavily defended; and, besides, the whole Russian Baltic fleet is anchored in the immediate vicinity, in and outside the harbour. We in the leading staff aircraft always fly at an altitude between 9000 and 10,000 feet; that is very low but, after all, we want to hit something. When diving on to the ships we use our diving brakes in order to check our diving speed. This gives us more time to sight the target and to correct our aim. The more carefully we aim, the better the results of our attack, and everything depends on them. By reducing our diving speed we make it easier for the flak to bring us down, especially as if

Stuka ace Hans-Ulrich Rudel, who sank the battleship Marat.
(Bundesarchiv)

we do not overshoot we cannot climb so fast after the dive. But, unlike the flights behind us, we do not generally try to climb back out of the dive. We use different tactics and pull out at low level close above the water. We have then to take the wildest evasive action over the enemy occupied coastal strip. Once we have left it behind we can breathe freely again.

The *Luftwaffe* War Diaries (Cajus Bekker) records that:

On September 22nd Major Trautloft, Kommodore of JG 54, based at Siverskaya, made an excursion to the Leningrad front. He wanted for once to examine the city closely through a telescope from the ground. For a fort-night his Messerschmitts had been circling over it, usually at high altitude because of the flak, which was worse than anything they had experienced over London. The air was alive with metal, especially over the Bay of Kronstadt, where the red Fleet lay at anchor. The Messerschmitts, as escort to bombers raiding the city, had tangled daily with Russian Curtisses and Ratas.[The 'Curtisses' were actually I-15s and the Ratas I-16s. Rata –rat – was a nickname bestowed on the Polikarpov fighter in the Spanish civil war – author].

Through the artillery spotter's telescope Leningrad's church towers, palaces and high blocks of flats seemed almost near enough to touch. But the city was on fire from one end to the other. High above the German outpost a force of Stukas dived down on the Russian warships for the third time that day. Fascinated, Trautloft watched as the twenty or thirty machines turned almost together and went down to face the flak.

At that moment a voice shouted: "Take cover, Herr Major, we are under attack!"

Six Curtisses closed in on the German post, their guns producing a shower of splinters. Finding himself for once in the position of a front-line infantryman, the fighter commander reacted in precisely the same way: "Where the hell," he demanded from the artillery officer lying beside him, "are our fighters?"

It was the more humiliating inasmuch as, thousands of feet above, his Messerschmitts could be seen glinting in the sun. The Army officer said with a grin: "You should know, Herr Major, that all available machines have been ordered by Corps to confine themselves to escorting the Stukas!"

Henceforth Trautloft knew what it was like to be attacked by enemy planes while watching one's own air force apparently engaged on a pleasure flight . . .

On 23 September, Rudel hit the *Marat* with a single 2200lb bomb, destroying the whole of her bow, including 'A' turret. The warship settled on an even keel in very shallow water, with her hull and super-structure both above the surface. As her machinery and both aft turrets were still operative, she continued in use as a beached gun battery. Later, 'B' turret, which had been damaged in the attack, was also brought back into action.

In other attacks, *Oktyabrskaya Revolutsiya* managed to escape severe damage, but took hits from six medium bombs. The intense air bombardment was maintained for three days, in the course of which the destroyer *Steregushchi* capsized after a direct hit (she was later salvaged), and the destroyers *Gordi, Grozyaschi* and *Silny* were damaged, along with the submarine depot ship *Smolny* and the submarine Shch-306. On 23 September, *Maksim Gorki*, already hit during an attack on Leningrad, was damaged again, as were *Kirov* and *Grozyaschi* off Krontstadt. The submarine P2 was destroyed in the dockyard, and the flotilla leader *Minsk* sank after a direct hit (she, too, was later salvaged). The patrol ship *Taifun* was destroyed, and the submarine Shch-302 damaged.

The attack on the *Kirov* cost the life if III/St.G.2's commander, Captain Ernst-Siegfried Steen, and his gunner, Corporal Alfred Scharnovski, who was normally Rudel's second crew member. According to eyewitnesses, Steen's aircraft was hit by flak in the dive and the pilot tried to steer it into the cruiser, but crashed and exploded in the water nearby.

As an insurance against the failure of the air attacks, and the possi-bility that the Baltic Fleet might attempt to break out of Kronstadt, the German Baltic Fleet under Vice-Admiral Ciliax deployed to the Aaland Sea, in the northern region of the Baltic. A powerful battle squadron was involved, comprising the battleship *Tirpitz,* the heavy cruiser *Admiral Scheer*, the cruisers *Köln* and *Nürnberg*, the destroyers Z25, Z26 and Z27 and five torpedo-boats forming a northern group, while the cruisers *Emden* and *Leipzig,* together with some S-boats, were held in reserve at Libau. When the air attacks proved successful, these forces were with-drawn to Gotenhafen on 29 September.

By this time, Leningrad itself was under constant air and artillery bombardment. The first long-range artillery shell had fallen on the city on 1 September. The bombardment that followed was persistent rather than intensive, but a number of industrial targets, including one of the power stations supplying Leningrad with electricity, were hit during the first week, and in one *Luftwaffe* attack on 8 September 178 fires were started.

The population of Leningrad at the beginning of the siege was about 2,500,000, but this had been swollen by an additional 100,000 refugees, fleeing ahead of the German invasion forces. The entire Baltic fleet was also dependent on the city's resources. The fleet could not move because of the necessity to defend the city on the west, and the refugees could not be evacuated because the German siege perimeter around the city now formed an impenetrable barrier.

The food situation was bad enough. On 12 September, there were stockpiles of flour sufficient for 35 days, cereals for 30 days, meat for 33 days, fats for 45 days and sugar for 60 days, and even these were constantly being diminished by German air attacks. On 7 September, for example enemy bombs hit a warehouse and 2500 tons of sugar went up in flames. Later, in still more desperate times, the solidified, ash-encrusted syrup was recovered and turned into confectionary. 'It tasted,' said one citizen, 'like burnt rubber flavoured with nail varnish, and it contained lumps of wood ash that had eluded the filtering process. But I suppose it had some nutritional value. The point was, they'd added some gum Arabic to it so that it lasted a long time in the mouth, like chewing gum, and therefore encouraged saliva and the impression that you'd been eating something.'

Hunger was not the only misery that had to be endured by the people of Leningrad. Bureaucracy and incompetence bedevilled their existence, and the air was laden with political rhetoric that did nothing to fill empty stomachs. Even those responsible for the defence of the city had to put up with the ranting of political commissars, who were not above over-riding sensible orders and replacing them with foolish ones. The general inefficiency that riddled the city's administration often resulted in farcical situations. Before the rail links between Moscow and Leningrad were severed, for example, trains that might profitably have been used to bring food supplies to Leningrad instead brought supplies of raw materials and ammunition from Moscow – while trains filled with exactly the same materials left Leningrad, bound for the Moscow front.

During October and November the food stocks continued to dwindle. The weather grew steadily colder. Buses were taken off the road for lack of fuel, and tramcars were restricted according to the amount of coal available to produce electricity at the power stations. No electric heating of any kind was allowed in private houses of apartment blocks. Telephones were disconnected. Kerosene for oil lamps was rationed, then withdrawn from public sale.

Within the city, the great hunger grew. It was especially bad for the army of citizens who had been mobilised to build the city's lines of defence, and for those engaged in other forms of hard manual labour, such as felling trees for fuel. In the words of the Russian writer Aleksandr Karasev:

On 8 October the City and Provincial Committees put into operation plans for cutting timber in the Pargolovo and Vsevolozhsk areas north of the city. The wood-cutting teams consisted mostly of women and adolescents; they arrived in the woods without proper tools or clothing and there was no housing or transport accommodation for them. The whole plan was threatened with collapse. By late October only one per cent of the plan had been fulfilled. In one area only a quarter of the eight hundred people were working. Wearing only light shoes and overcoats and suffering from hunger and cold these girls nevertheless did wonders. Working in forty degrees of frost they laid down a track to the nearest railway line, built barracks to house themselves, and delivered substantial quantities of timber to the city.

On 9 November the Germans captured the town of Tikhvin, and with it the vital railhead, the only supply point for the entire city. Not only the railhead was lost; so was the airhead, a small airfield into which Soviet Air Force Lisunov Li-2 transports (licence-built versions of the American Douglas DC-3 airliner) had been flying in supplies on a relatively small scale. Now Leningrad was truly isolated. The next nearest railway station was Zaborie, sixty miles farther east than Tikhvin, and it would be virtually impossible to establish a link with it. The country to the east of Lake Ladoga and north of the German-held salient was almost entirely swamp and forest, with no road through it, and in any case it was isolated from Osinovets on the south-west shore of the lake by the lake itself, now frozen over and impassable to water traffic. Even if a road could be built from the east side of the narrowest part of the lake – Schlusselburg Bay – to Zaborie it would still have to be linked with Osinovets if it was to serve any purpose.

In time, the lake would freeze solidly enough to permit the passage of heavy traffic across its surface, but that would not occur until mid-January, and in the meantime people were beginning to die of cold and starvation.

Shortly after the fall of Tikhvin in November, the City Council issued the following announcement in the newspaper Leningradskaya Pravda:

The administration does not hide the truth from the people. With the temporary loss of the town of Tikhvin there can be no hope of an early improvement in the supply situation. General Meretskov and his heroic soldiers of the Red Army are battling for their lives and for ours and their heroism will surely be rewarded by the return of Tikhvin to Soviet hands. Meanwhile your Comrades in the administration have decided that a route across the ice of Lake Ladoga must be found and a road extended eastward for the two hundred miles that divide our city from Zaborie. Only by the construction of such a route can there be any hope of supplies reaching us.

The road will be begun as soon as the the slightest chance of the adequate weight bearing capacity of the lake is reported by our scientists.

First, there had to be a reconnaissance of the route. At six o'clock in the morning of 18 November, 1941, a small party assembled in the ruins of Osinovets. It comprised four Party officials, a glaciologist from the Admiralty, and an undernourished horse. Each man carried two days' rations – half a pound of bread, a single slice of pressed meat, and a bar of chocolate. The horse carried two panniers containing evergreen leaves – its fodder for the journey.

The task of the party was to cross the bay to the village of Lednevo, a distance of about twenty miles, marking out a route where the ice was thick enough to bear the weight of a horse-drawn sleigh carrying 224 pounds – one tenth of a ton – of supplies. To test the concept, two men would sit on the sleigh, which was harnessed to the emaciated horse, while the others went on ahead to test the thickness of the ice.

The party set off into the teeth of a blizzard, the walking men linked to one another by thin cords. Every fifteen minutes the glaciologist would bore a hole in the ice to take depth measurements, and if these were satisfactory he would insert a marker rod into the hole. Somehow, at the limit of their endurance, they completed their task, reaching Lednevo in the afternoon of 20 November after a journey of some sixty hours, most of it with the blizzard still raging. Their reconnaissance was duly recorded in the records of the Leningrad Military Council, but its epic nature was forgotten.

On 21 November, the Leningrad Military Council, having received the reconnaissance party's report by radio, dispatched ten light trucks across the ice to Lednevo. Eight arrived, the other two having got lost in a snow-storm and fallen though thin ice. On the 24th, the eight surviving trucks returned to Leningrad, carrying thirty-three tons of supplies – one-hundredth of the city's minimum daily requirement.

At Lednevo, the military authorities began assembling the army of workers necessary to extend the supply road to Zaborie. Already, it was becoming known as the Road of Life. Work went on around the clock. It absorbed the efforts of thousands of men, women and children, soldiers and civilians, clearing a path through the forests, laying down fascines across swamps and minor rivers, working with no more than picks and shovels to mark the route and handsaws to fell trees. Sometimes, tractors were used to haul timber when petrol could be found for them, but mostly the work was done by hard physical labour, sustained only by an ounce of two of bread or a piece of raw swede or potato. Countless died of cold, hunger and over-exertion, their bodies buried under the Road of Life itself.

The whole road was in fact no more than a makeshift track running between banks of shovelled snow, filled with pitfalls, liable to cave in if the temperature rose and the fascines sank into the sodden ground. But it was road of sorts, over which trucks could be driven in single file, and on 6 December 1941 it burst at last from the forest, almost within sight of Zaborie. The first convoy of trucks was already waiting, and it was on its way to Leningrad within minutes of the road being completed.

In his book The Siege of Leningrad, Alan Wykes describes that first nightmare journey.

Three hours after it was started the convoy was halted because the leading truck was stuck in the snow. The road was so narrow that nothing could get round it and there was a delay while it was dug out. That delay was repeated innumerable times throughout the long journey. Not only the depth of the snow, but also the steepness of the hills, the long stretches of inadequately forded swamp, continuing blizzards, enemy shelling, and the unfamiliar country, all contrived hazards that led to chaos and the loss of many trucks. The maximum distance travelled by the convoy in any one day was twenty miles, and it was often only half that. When eventually the ragged remnants of the convoy reached Lednevo six days had passed; and the slow crossing of the lake, with every truck's speed reduced to a crawl to avoid breaking the still frail ice, took another twenty-seven hours. Throughout the two hundred miles between Leningrad and the railhead at Zaborie the road was littered with broken down or trapped trucks – more than three hundred and fifty of them. The immense labour of building the Lifeline Road had resulted in the arrival of rather less than a day's supplies.

It was a beginning; but the great irony was that on 9 December, three days after the road had been completed, with all its human sacrifice, Soviet forces recaptured the railhead at Tikhvin, although it would be some time before the effect of this was felt. In the meantime, the population of Leningrad continued to starve. Alan Wykes gives a horrifying account of their sufferings:

There were no Goyas or Picassos in Leningrad; but Kochergin's painting By the Fence of the Summer Garden depicts in terrible simplicity a single aspect of the city's suffering. Behind the elegant railings of the park the trees are laden with snow and in the foreground on the pavement one body lies supine and another is crouched in the angle of a buttress. Death has overtaken both these anonymous Leningraders. That is the way it was. People went on their journeys without the strength to complete them and thousands of them collapsed in the streets. Soon the snow drifted over them and they were not seen again until the spring thaw; those who saw them fall could give no help – and might themselves collapse a few steps later . . .

People who died in their homes had to lie there until a band of relations or neighbours with enough aggregate strength to carry them could be summoned. There was no wood available for coffins and there was no space in the cemeteries. Mass graves were opened in bombed sites by explosives and bodies were simply tipped into them. The main sewage systems were bombed and could not be repaired for lack of materials and workers, and the accumulation of excrement, refuse and dead bodies in the streets or open graves was a continual threat to health. But the bitter cold mercifully counteracted the effects of the decay of flesh and filth and there were no serious epidemics.

Amid all the misery, the factories in Leningrad and its environs within the siege perimeter continued to function. Russian writer Aleksandr Fedeyev was an eyewitness to the dedication of the workers.

When the Germans approached Kolpino (located on a tributary of the Neva about sixteen miles south-east of Leningrad – author) the workers of the Izhorsky plant took a vow not to yield either the factory or the town; the Germans would have to force a passage over their dead bones. In the result the front came right up to Kolpino itself. The town and the factory were subjected to systematic assault from the air and to an artillery bombardment which went on without pause day and night. Several generations of Izhorsky people, from infants at the breast to the most ancient men and women, were represented among those killed by bomb or shell fragments. But Kolpino remained in the hands of the Izhorsky workers, and the factory, in spite of everything, went on producing.

Much of Kolpino is ruins. When I was with Lieutenant-Colonel Shubin at the artillery observation post, the enemy's field guns were methodically, remorselessly and senselessly pounding the little wooden houses and huts. Our forward line was a few kilometres in front of us, almost on the edge of the town; the firing there was particularly heavy. But the peacetime ways of the town had not altogether ceased. Women did their washing at the pond. Two girls at the crossroads chatted and laughed. An old woman in a black dress walked slowly along the road, carrying in her arms a grandchild a few months old. The infant slept.

In Leningrad, hordes of rats, starving like the people above ground, emerged into the streets and paid the price, being quickly caught, skinned and roasted or made into stews. Cats, dogs and birds went the same way. Horses that dropped dead in their traces were cut up on the spot and the meat that remained on their bones was collected for 'processing'. The word applied to anything that could remotely be considered edible, as Alan Wykes records:

> Books were stripped of their covers and the glue in the bindings melted down as an ingredient for soup; hair oil was drunk in lieu of fat; the intestines of the rats, cats and other creatures that died or were killed to make a glutinous jelly that was spread on bread whenever there was any bread to spread it on; dried evergreen leaves were stewed as a herbal broth; wallpaper was stripped from walls and the residue of dried paste used as an admixture with flour; the bones of dead animals – and possibly humans – were stewed for hours on fires kept going with books, letters and anything else flammable, in the hope of extracting a little marrow from them; yeast was turned into soup and soap into jelly . . .
>
> Cellulose bread, glue soup, rat-offal jelly, seaweed milk: the list of food substitutes that were contrived reads like some hell-hags' banquet. But if they gave no nourishment – which of course they didn't – they gave an illusion of brief satisfaction. A more real and more terrible satisfaction was gained from the eating of the human flesh – what there was of it – of those who had died.

Another historian, Leon Goure, who wrote a history of the siege, quotes eye-witness accounts and German documents that refer to cannibalism.

> Most instances appear to have involved the mutilation or dismemberment of corpses found in the streets or stored in the morgues before they were removed to the cemeteries. It was rumoured that some of the meat obtained in this fashion was sold in the black market in exchange for more conventional food or resellable objects, but sometimes the despoilers ate it themselves. There were even said to be crazed parents eating their children, and vice versa.

The horrors in Leningrad were compounded by the sick and wounded who were brought back from the front, usually on carts dragged by people. A medical student wrote:

> It took seven hours on one occasion to get two hundred dying militiamen from the street to the upper floor of the hospital. The hospital itself was like

The T-34 tank eventually turned the tide of armoured warfare on the eastern front, but was only available in small numbers early in the campaign. This example has fallen victim to an 88mm anti-tank gun.

> *some ghastly picture of a medieval torture chamber. The temperature in the wards was usually about 30 degrees F. The patients lay fully clothed, with coats and blankets, and sometimes even mattresses, piled on top of them. The walls were covered with frost. During the night water froze in the pitchers. The hunger had the effect of causing diarrhoea among the patients, many of whom from weakness were unable to use the bed-pans. Sheets on the beds were filthy – no water for laundering. The only medicine available was sodium bromide, and the doctors prescribed it to the patients under various names . . . All the baths and bed-pans were filled with excrement and refuse, all of which froze on the spot. The medical staff could barely stand on their feet through hunger, cold and overwork.*

In November 1941 the death toll in Leningrad was eleven thousand. In December, it rose to fifty thousand. Yet the recapture of Tikhvin, which cost the Germans 7000 dead and pushed back the front in this sector fifty miles westward to the far side of the Volkhov river, brought a surge of hope, even though the task that lay ahead was daunting. The first priority was to rebuild the railway bridges carrying the line from Tikhvin to Volkhov and on to Leningrad, all of which had been destroyed in the fighting.

By the end of the year, thanks to the restored railway, the forest road and the tenuous passage across the unpredictable ice of Lake Ladoga, it became possible to increase the city's bread ration slightly, and to evacuate some of the worst cases of sickness. It was becoming apparent that Hitler's plan to starve Leningrad into submission, abandoning any idea of a direct assault on the city in order to divert available forces to Army Group Centre's drive on Moscow, was not going to work. Moreover, the German forces surrounding the city were being subjected to increasingly ferocious, if as yet limited, Russian counter-attacks, supported by a new 28-ton tank armed with a 76mm gun. The Russians called it the T-34.

CHAPTER TEN

1942:
The Russian Recovery

In December 1941, Adolf Hitler, enraged by the stubborn failure of the citizens of Leningrad to capitulate, replaced Field Marshal von Leeb with Colonel-General von Küchler, who received the following directive:

> *The Führer orders that Petersburg be wiped off the face of the earth. After the defeat of Soviet Russia, there will be no purpose in the further existence of this large inhabited locality . . . It is proposed to blockade the city by continuous artillery fire of all calibres and to raze it to the ground by air bombardment. If the situation compels the city to propose surrender, such proposals shall be rejected.*

As a direct consequence of this order, Leningrad was subjected to artillery bombardment on 252 days during 1942, during the course of which the Germans fired 50,000 shells into the city. The *Luftwaffe* also continued its bombing campaign, although the growing competence of the Soviet fighter pilots, and the availability of new aircraft types, inflicted growing losses on the enemy. Aid from Britain and America was arriving in the ports of North Russia; it included aircraft types like the Curtiss P-40 Warhawk, the Bell P-39 Airacobra and the Hawker Hurricane. Some of the latter were issued to the 3rd Fighter Regiment of the Soviet Baltic Fleet, operating in the Leningrad sector, the Russian pilots, used to the much lighter Yaks and LaGGs, viewing it with mixed feelings.

> *I thought that the name 'Hurricane' hardly marched the technical quali-ties of the machine,* wrote Lieutenant Viktor Kaberov. *The armament*

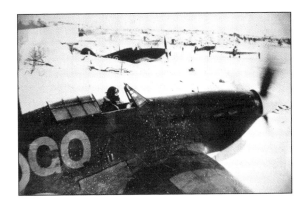

The first Hawker Hurricane fighters to reach the Soviet Union were aircraft of No 151 Wing RAF, which deployed to Murmansk in 1941. (IWM)

on it was now good – two 20mm cannons and two heavy calibre machine guns. One burst and pieces would fly off any aircraft. The armour plating (taken from our LaGG) was fine. Such protection was like a stone wall. The horizon indicator was also a wonderful instrument. It was easy to fly in the clouds with it. The radio worked perfectly, like a domestic telephone: neither noise nor crackle. But the speed, the speed . . . No, this aircraft was far from being a Hurricane. It was slow to gain height and was not good in a dive. As for vertical manoeuvrability – not good at all!

Shortcomings or not, it was aircraft like the Hurricane that helped the Soviet fighter pilots to hold their own against the *Luftwaffe* in 1942, a year that saw the appearance in large numbers of a Soviet combat type, the Ilyushin Il-2 Shturmovik. The requirements that led to the development of the Il-2 were summed up by its designer, Sergei Ilyushin, who later wrote:

A Hawker Hurricane in Russian markings. (IWM)

My task was to build an aircraft which could be used effectively in support of our ground forces. The main function of such an aircraft would therefore be the destruction of enemy ground forces, that is to say infantry, tanks, trucks, artillery, fortifications and so on. For this purpose, the aircraft would have to be capable of carrying a varied weapon-load of machine guns, cannon, bombs and rockets.

In order to seek out and attack targets as small as tanks and trucks, camouflaged into the bargain, the aircraft would have to operate at very low altitude, between 50 and 500 feet. But this would mean that the aircraft would be subjected to concentrated enemy ground fire, and consequently it would need to be very heavily armoured. Evidently it would be impossible to protect the aircraft against every kind of enemy weapon, and this left me with a serious problem: what type of armour to choose. In the end, I settled for armour-plating of a thickness which, while providing sufficient protection against small-calibre weapons, would not result in a sacrifice of performance

Altogether, 249 Il-2s were built during 1941, but production was drastically curtailed by the removal of the factories to the safe areas of the eastern USSR. Also, the early-model Il-2s were single-seater, with no rear defensive armament, and suffered heavy losses to enemy fighters. In 1942 it was replaced on the production line by a two-seat version, with a rear gun position, and after that the combination of Il-2 assault aircraft and T-34 tank became a formidable one.

In the middle of January 1942, the Russians – encouraged by their successful defence of Moscow, and with their front-line forces reinforced by fresh combat divisions from Siberia – launched a major offensive on the Kalinin front with the aim of encircling Army Group Centre. In bitter

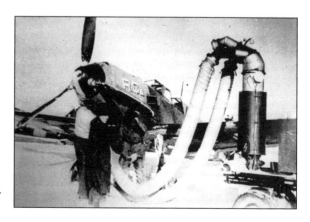

The Russian winter caused serious problems for German equipment. This device was employed to pump warm air round the engine of a Messerschmitt Bf 109. (Author's collection)

cold and deep snow, the Third and Fourth Shock Armies, driving through the Valday Hills to the north of Rzhev, hammered a wedge between Army Group North and Army Group Centre. On the western front, the Russians advanced along the Smolensk Highway and recaptured Mozhaisk. To the south, the Soviet Thirty-third Army launched a strong thrust towards Vyazma, and on 20 January the 4th Airborne Corps was dropped to the south of this town by an armada of transport aircraft.

On the north-western front, the situation of the German Ninth Army – denied reinforcements from the west by the Soviet thrust through Mozhaisk, was becoming desperate. By early February, 100,000 men – six divisions in total – were completely surrounded at Demyansk, south-east of Lake Ilmen. On 20 February the Germans mustered every available Junkers Ju 52 transport aircraft, 75 in all, and began airlifting supplies into the Demyansk pocket. Initially, the transports made the trips in ones and twos, but to reach Demyansk they had to fly 100 miles over enemy territory and the Russians quickly set up a formidable flak corridor along their route. Apart from the flak, there were the fighters; when the weather permitted, the Russians maintained standing patrols over Demyansk, and the lumbering Ju 52s were easy game for the MiGs and LaGGs. As losses began to mount the transports were forced to make the flight in close formation, with strong fighter escort, and – mainly because the Russian fighter pilots had received orders to avoid combat with the Messerschmitts and concentrate on the transports – the situation improved slightly. Even so, operating conditions were fearful, and after three weeks only a quarter of the transport force remained serviceable. The airlift continued, however, and for three months, until a narrow supply route was opened by the Germans in May, the transports flew in over 24,000 tons of supplies.

During the operation, the *Luftwaffe* lost 265 machines, the majority being written off accidentally on airfields covered in snow and ice. Supplies were also airlifted to a second German pocket at Kholm; conditions here were even more difficult, for the airstrip was within range of Russian artillery. After a few weeks the Junkers 52s had suffered such crippling losses that they were unable to continue operating, and supplies had to be dropped by parachute from bomber aircraft or landed by glider. On many occasions, fierce battles developed between the Germans and Russians for supplies that fell in no-man's land. In spite of everything, the supplies kept the 3500 troops in the pocket going until they were relieved early in May. The success of these airlifts, under the most adverse conditions, helped to convince *Luftwaffe* C-in-C Hermann Göring that the *Luftwaffe* alone could keep large garrisons of German

Reichsmarschall Herman Göring, seen here addressing Luftwaffe *fighter pilots, boasted that his transport fleet could supply encircled German forces.* (Bundesarchiv)

troops supplied, even in the face of stiff resistance. It was a dangerous assumption, as events at Stalingrad later in that fateful year of 1942 were to show.

Although it drove deep wedges into German-held territory, the Soviet winter offensive of 1942 failed in its primary aims. Notwithstanding desperate Soviet assaults, strongly fortified centres of German resistance, mainly at Staraya Russa, Demidov, Velizh and Velikiye Luki, held out until the spring thaw, under constant bombardment by artillery and the Soviet Air Force. And the blockade of Leningrad remained in place, although water traffic over Lake Ladoga would soon resume with the thaw, as Aleksandr Fedeyev observed:

> *All my life I shall preserve the memory of that evening towards the end of April 1942, when our plane, escorted by fighters, flew very low over Lake Ladoga and beneath us, on the ice, which was cracked and fissured, with surging tides of water in between, stretched the road, the only road, which throughout the winter had linked Leningrad with the rest of the country . . . It had already been torn to shreds – virtually obliterated – and in places was a mere flood of water. The plane flew straight through the misty, crimson, diffuse globe of the sun, which caught the tops of the pines and*

firs along the entire length of the lakeshore behind us in the tender glow of spring.

The rations, although increased, were still austere, as Fedeyev discovered during this visit to Leningrad in the spring of 1942.

When I entered the room my cousin, who had a friend with her, a woman as emaciated as herself, was having her dinner. Because of the increased rations for the First of May, their dinner, judged by Leningrad standards, might have been called luxurious. It included even beer and vodka prepared from dried orange rind. Among the dishes was the famous Leningrad-blockade jelly – a jelly made from carpenter's glue. Here was the reverse process: you cooked the glue, removed all the bone scum – or, rather, the scum of what had once been bone – and added gelatine to the rest. Then you let it cool. The jelly was absolutely tasteless and its nutritive value was dubious, but it was a stay and comfort for many people in Leningrad.

By the end of 1942 the days of complete German air superiority on the Leningrad front were over, and although some of the Russian equipment was still outmoded, the Soviet pilots fought fierce battles against their German and Finnish opponents. One of the latter was air ace Eino Luukkanen, who described one hectic air fight. The Finnish pilots were flying Brewster Buffaloes.

Foul weather. Day after day of low cloud, rain and dank mist kept the squadron grounded at Rompotti, our spirits as grey as the skies sitting on the tops of the surrounding trees. The days passed in dreary succession, the tedium fraying both nerves and tempers, but at last, on October 30, 1942, after nearly a month of kicking our heels on the ground, the ceiling lifted and we took off into a grey dawn on an offensive patrol with five planes.

Reiska Valli's oil pump began to give trouble soon after take-off, so he was forced to abort, leaving four of us to continue southward. The horizon was indistinct and visibility was not too good, but Vaffe Vahvelainen, one of our flight sergeants who was taking a turn of duty at the Seivasto radio warning station, called us over the radio, directing us toward an enemy formation that had been spotted south of the station. I scanned the sky thoroughly and above the Inkeri shoreline, near Oranienbaum on the Russian side, and well above our altitude I counted eight tiny black specks. I called my companions, pointing out the Russians above us, and suggested that we might take on two each!

We began climbing towards the enemy formation, the needle of the altimeter slowly unwinding. Eight . . . nine . . . ten . . . eleven thousand feet. At this altitude we could see that six of the Russians were I-16s, but the other two fighters were not so readily identifiable. Twelve . . . thirteen thousand feet, and it was obvious that the Russians had spotted us. There was no longer any chance of bouncing them so, with throttles wide open, we tore into the Ivans, each selecting a target. I fired one short burst at an I-16 and pulled up into an Immelmann [a stall turn, devised by the World War One German ace Max Immelmann, designed to bring a fighter down on an opponent's tail – author]. The sky was immediately a fantastic melee of frantically twisting and turning aircraft. The intercom was a babble of excited voices, oaths, warnings, and counter-warnings. The third flight was operating on the same wavelength and had evidently taken a large gaggle of Russians somewhere near Seiskari. Everyone was shouting at the same time. Above me, an I-16 clawed into a vertical stall, stood on its tail, for a fraction of a second, and then fell away into the forest below. Almost at the same moment tracers flickered past my cockpit. Instinctively, with throttle wide open, I pulled the Brewster into the tightest of shuddering vertical turns, and the I-16 that had managed to get on to my tail flashed past and was gone.

Out of the corner of my eye I spotted one of our Brewsters far below with a Spitfire on his tail. So that was what the two unidentified fighters had been – Spitfires. There was no mistaking the curved wings of the graceful British fighter, and this was the first time we had encountered the type in Russian hands. I yawed the tail of my Brewster to make sure that no Ivan was stealing up on me, and then, stick over and well forward, I plunged down in a near-vertical dive. I fired one long burst into the cockpit of the Spitfire which immediately flicked over on its back and dived straight into the sea near the village of Karavalda, on the Gulf. [In fact, the Russian fighter could not have been a Spitfire, which was not delivered to the Russians until early in 1943. It must have been a Hurricane, or possibly a Yak-1 – author].

With the major units of the Baltic Fleet crippled by air attack, submarines remained the Russians' only hope of prosecuting a naval war in the theatre, and in the spring of 1942, as the ice was beginning to clear, the Red Banner Feet prepared its submarines for a breakout through the Finnish-German minefields into the open Baltic. The boats were given a thick coat of paint, presumably in the hope that it would give some sort of protection against magnetic mines and sound detection apparatus, and wooden frames around hydroplanes and other projections were fitted to supplement the standard jumping wires for brushing aside mine-mooring cables. Submarine commanders were ordered to try to avoid minefields altogether by keeping to shallow water and, if this proved impossible, to pass beneath suspected minefields at as great a depth as possible.

Between 12 and 19 June 1942, five submarines set out to traverse the 'Seeigel' mine barrage in the vicinity of Lavansaari Island, losing M-95 east of Suusaari en route. The remainder operated in the eastern Baltic, where they succeeded in sinking a dozen merchant ships – three of which, unfortunately, were flying the flag of neutral Sweden. Most of the damage was done by S-7 and S-317, which accounted for four ships each. Despite these genuine successes, the claims of the Soviet submarine commanders were often greatly exaggerated. For example, two further Baltic sorties, in August and September 1942, resulted in claims of fourteen merchant vessels of 100,000 tons sunk in total, whereas the actual tally was five ships of 10,000 tons total. The Russians, for their part, lost two submarines, with another severely damaged by mines.

Eighteen boats were sent out between 18 September and early November 1942, with disastrous results; four were mined in passage and three more were sunk by Finnish submarines. The Russians claimed eighteen enemy vessels totalling 150,000 tons sunk; the actual figure was six ships of 12,000 tons. However, with 400,000 troops passing through the Baltic in 1942, the Germans could not afford to ignore the underwater threat, and early in 1943 the *Kriegsmarine*, assisted by the Finnish Navy, laid more minefields in the Gulf of Finland. In April, the western end of the Gulf was completely sealed by a double anti-submarine net, which proved impenetrable. Soviet submarines were entirely prevented from operating in the Baltic until 4 September 1944, when Finland and the Soviet Union effected a truce and the Finns were obliged to clear a way through the defences close to the Finnish coastline.

In the southern part of the Baltic, the German naval presence had been much diminished. The battleship *Tirpitz* had gone; after her period as flagship of the Baltic Fleet in the autumn of 1941 she had passed through the Kiel Canal to her home port of Wilhelmshaven, and from there, on the night of 16 January 1942, flying the flag of Admiral Ciliax and under the command of Captain Topp, she had sailed for Norwegian waters, never to return.

Shortly after this, the Germans received a foretaste of things to come when RAF Bomber Command conducted what was described as an 'experiment', involving a saturation attack on an enemy city with incendiary bombs instead of high explosive. The target was Lübeck, the ancient and beautiful port city at the gateway to the Baltic, selected because many of its buildings were old and inflammable and its streets

The battleship Tirpitz, *photographed in a Norwegian fjord by a Royal Air Force reconnaissance aircraft.* (IWM)

narrow, affording good conditions for the development of firestorms. The centre of Lübeck – the Altstadt – was also densely populated, containing some thirty thousand people. Another ninety thousand lived in the suburbs.

On the night of 28/29 March, 1942, 234 aircraft set out for this target, most of them carrying incendiaries. The final wave, which was to attack an hour after the main force, consisted of forty-seven Vickers Wellingtons and eighteen Avro Manchesters carrying high explosives, including 4000lb 'blockbuster' bombs. A total of 191 aircraft claimed to have attacked the target, and the raid was a complete success. Two hundred acres of the city were destroyed, mainly by fire, and there was additional heavy damage in the suburbs. The raid caused considerable panic, not only among the population of Lübeck and the surrounding area but also among the German administration in Berlin. It was thirty-two hours before the last fires were put out. One thousand dwellings were destroyed and 4000 damaged; 320 civilians were killed and 785 injured. Eight bombers were shot down, mostly by night fighters on the way home.

The activities of the Fleet Training Squadron, meanwhile, continued unhindered, and at the end of 1942, although Germany was beginning to suffer reverses on the Russian steppes and in North Africa, the war seemed very far away. Early in 1943 the heavy cruiser *Admiral Scheer* arrived in the Baltic, fresh from active service in Norway, and a few weeks later the arrival of another warship at Stettin, virtually complete but not quite, caused quite a stir. She was the aircraft carrier *Graf Zeppelin*, whose construction programme had been resumed in 1942 but once again halted. She reached Stettin under tow from Kiel, and no one quite knew what was to become of her.

Very few people, either, knew exactly what was going on at a curious and very secret establishment at a remote spot on the southern shore of the Baltic, miles from anywhere. Its name was Peenemünde.

PART FOUR

The Turning of the Tide

CHAPTER ELEVEN

Secret Weapons and Air Battles

U nder the terms of the Treaty of Versailles, Germany was forbidden to possess or manufacture long-range artillery. During the First World War her primary armaments manufacturer, Krupp, had produced guns capable of throwing a one-ton shell over a distance of ten miles, and Allied delegates at Versailles recalled how the biggest gun of all, nicknamed 'Big Bertha', had smashed the forts of Liège, Maubeuge and Antwerp.

Casting around for an alternative to long-range artillery, some future was seen in rocketry, and the task of investigating this area was given to Reichswehr Captain Walter Dornberger in 1929. At that time, Dornberger was on a five-year attachment to the Technical University of Charlottenburg, studying physics.

In 1932, Dornberger was approached by members of the *Verein für Raumschiffahrt* (VfR, Spaceflight Society) amateur rocketry group, who were looking for funding, and he agreed to attend a demonstration. The launch of a liquid-fuelled rocket designed by the group was a failure, the device exploding on its launch pad. Even so, Dornberger was impressed with the group and with his contact, Wernher von Braun, and offered them a contract to work on secret rocket weapons for the army. The group declined the offer, but von Braun himself agreed to work for Dornberger. The young scientist joined Dornberger's team at the army's Kummersdorf firing range, fifteen miles south of Berlin, in 1933, as soon as he had graduated from the Berlin Technical High School.

The army team's first complete liquid-fuelled rocket, the four-and-a-half foot long A1 (Aggregat-1), never flew, as it was found to be nose-heavy, but it was redesigned as the A2, and in December 1934 two of these were launched to an altitude of about 8000 feet from the North Sea island of Borkum.

As the scope of the work expanded and larger rockets were contemplated, it became obvious that a larger and more discreet testing range would be needed, Borkum being only an interim alternative to the usuitable Kummersdorf range. While Dornberger concentrated on securing ongoing funding for the experiments, von Braun searched for a secure location, preferably in a remote spot on the north German coast. In December 1935, while spending Christmas with relatives near the Baltic coast, he was reminded that his father had once hunted duck on the swampy island of Usedom, not far from a fishing village called Peenemünde. Walter Dornberger came to inspect it, and, as he recalled later, was highly impressed.

> *The place was far away from any large town or traffic of any kind, and consisted of dunes and marshland overgrown with ancient oaks and pines, nestling in untroubled solitude behind a reedy foreland reaching far out into smooth water. Big Pomerania deer with dark antlers roamed through the heather and among the bilberry bushes of the woods right to the sands of the low-lying coast. Swarms of duck, crested grebes, coots and swans inhabited this beautiful spot undisturbed for years by the report of the huntsman's shotgun. The bustle of the watering-places strung along the coast like a necklace of pearls never invaded the lonely islet of Peenemünde. I thought there would be no difficulty in building a railway and roads and concealing the really important installations in the woods. A small island . . . faced the Peene estuary, the Greifswalder Oie. There we could carry out our experiments unnoticed throughout the year. We had a range of over 250 miles eastwards along the Pomeranian coast.*

It was agreed that Peenemünde would be developed as Germany's principal rocket research establishment. The *Luftwaffe* would provide the basic installation and airfield, and the completed site would then be handed over to the army, who would supply the manpower and also be responsible for security. The eastern section of the site, designated Heeresversuchsanstalt Peenemünde (HVP), consisted of test beds and manufacturing facilities and was commanded by Colonel Leo Zanssen, Walter Dornberger being head of Weapon Test Section 11 and von Braun the technical director. The western section comprised the airfield and facilities for testing air-launched missiles, assisted take-off units and rocket-propelled aircraft, and was known as the *Eropbungstelle Karlshagen*, commanded by Major Henckelman.

Tests on a new experimental rocket, the 25-foot A3, were begun at

HVP in 1937. As Peenemünde was still under construction, the first launch took place from a makeshift pad on the adjacent island of Greifswalder Oie on 6 December that year and it was the first of four failures, the rockets losing stability and crashing after rising to an altitude of only a few hundred feet.

At this time a military rocket, the A4 (later to be known as the V2, the V standing for *Vergeltungswaffen*, or revenge weapon) was already under development, but work on this was halted while further experiments were carried out. The A3 was scrapped and a new research rocket, the A5, took its place. The A5, 22 feet long, used the same motor as the A3 but was fitted with new control surfaces, and had a more reliable gyroscopic control system developed by Siemens. The flight programme started in September 1938, with the launch of some inert one-fifth scale models from Heinkel He 111s at heights of up to 20,000 feet, the test vehicles being recovered from the Baltic following a parachute descent. Due to Siemens falling behind in their timetable, four full-size A5s without controls were launched from the Oie in July 1938 to verify the stability of the rocket, and although none reached supersonic speed, they all achieved stable flights of up to five miles. Gradually, stabilising and steering gear was perfected to give successful A5 flights of up to eleven miles range, ending in parachute descents.

With these successes to build on, design of the A4 resumed, but with a length of 46 feet the military rocket was twice as big as the A5, and to power it a new rocket motor producing over 55,000 pounds of thrust for sixty-eight seconds had to be developed, which required a basic amount of work and testing of various experimental units before the basic A4 motor emerged. Static firing of this basic motor began at Peenemünde on 21 March, 1940, but it was not until 18 March 1942 that a complete V2 assembly was statically tested, only to explode on the pad.

More embarrassing failures followed. The first V-2 test vehicle to be launched, on 13 June 1942, rose a few feet into the air, fell back on the launch pad and blew up, an electrical fault having caused the fuel pumps to fail. The second, on 16 August, broke up 45 seconds after launch while travelling at over Mach 3, its remains falling into the Baltic. Both failures occurred in front of visiting VIPs, who were not present on 3 October 1942, when the third launch took place. It was a pity, because this time the missile worked perfectly, flying 120 miles downrange along the Baltic coast to fall into the sea only two and a half miles from its predicted impact point. It reached an altitude of sixty miles and a speed of 3000 miles per hour.

Meanwhile, the Germans had been pursuing another high-priority

These photographs show the A4 (V2) rocket on its Meilerwagen *mobile launching platform, and just after launch.* (Author's collection)

programme at Peenemünde. It concerned a medium-range surface-to-surface flying bomb, officially known by the code-name *Kirschkern* (Cherrystone) and, for deception purposes, by the *Luftwaffe* designation FZG 76 (*Flakzielgerät* 76 or anti-aircraft aiming device 76). Its German Air Ministry designation was Fieseler Fi 103; it would soon become known to the world as the V1.

While work proceeded on the Argus pulse-jet that was to power the flying bomb, the Fieseler firm of Kassel developed the airframe, and in December 1942 the first unpowered Fi 103 was dropped from a Focke-Wulf Fw 200 parent aircraft over Peenemünde. On 25 December, an Fi 103 airframe was launched from a catapult assembly at Peenemünde-West and flew about 1000 yards. By the spring of 1943 the V1 had made many successful launches, and on 26 May a demonstration was held before a large collection of civilian and military VIPs to show off the capability of both V1 and V2, two examples of each missile being scheduled for launch. The two V1s both went out of control and crashed soon after leaving their launching ramps, but both V2s made successful flights, and two days later Dornberger was promoted to major-general in recognition of his efforts.

The Allies, meanwhile, were not unaware of what was happening at Peenemünde. Vague reports from agents in Poland to the effect that the Germans were developing novel long-range bombardment weapons were deemed worthy of further investigation, and the RAF began to send its long-range de Havilland Mosquito photo-reconnaissance aircraft to photograph areas of the Baltic coast. On 22 April 1943, Pilot Officer W.J. White set out in a Mosquito of No 540 Squadron to photograph Stettin and Politz, and decided to take a few shots of Peenemünde as well. Others were taken of Peenemünde on 2, 12 and 13 June. The prints were closely scrutinised, and revealed objects resembling large rockets.

The V1 flying bomb was, in effect, the world's first cruise missile. But it was inaccurate, and therefore classed as an area bombardment weapon.
(Author's collection)

On the night of 17/18 August, 1943, five hundred and ninety-seven heavy bombers set out from the bases of RAF Bomber Command to attack Peenemünde. The mission, which was code-named Operation Hydra, involved the precision bombing of a series of selected buildings grouped around three principal aiming points – the scientists' and workers' living quarters, the rocket factory and the experimental station. It was a difficult task, as the buildings were widely dispersed along the narrow coastal strip.

The operation was directed by Group Captain J.H. Searby of No 83 Squadron, Pathfinder Force, who remained over the target throughout the attack, passing instructions over the R/T to the main bomber force. It was the first time that the 'Master Bomber' technique was applied to a major attack. During the raid a new type of marker bomb was used; this was a 250-pounder crammed with impregnated cotton wool, which ignited at 3000 feet and burned with a brilliant crimson flame for about ten minutes. It was easily recognisable, and the Germans found it extremely difficult to devise an effective decoy.

The conditions were good, with bright moonlight, and Searby was able to control the raid successfully from start to finish, although there was one unfortunate incident when the initial marking and bombing fell on a labour camp for forced workers situated a mile and a half south of the first aiming point, but Searby quickly brought the situation under control. Thanks to a handful of Mosquitoes, which dropped masses of flares over Berlin, the German fighter controllers were led to believe that the capital was the target, and as a result 148 fighters patrolled overhead for the best part of a hour without sighting a single enemy aircraft. Five hundred and sixty aircraft attacked the target, dropping 1800 tons of bombs, most of which were high explosive. Approximately 180 Germans were killed in the attack, nearly all in the workers' accommodation area, and 500-600 foreigners, mostly Poles, were killed in the workers' camp, where they were housed in flimsy wooden barracks without the benefit of air-raid shelters.

Despite the deception over Berlin, Bomber Command lost forty aircraft that night, many of them falling victim to the so-called *Wilde Sau* (Wild Boar) tactics adopted by the *Luftwaffe*, in which fighters cruised at high altitude and looked for their bomber targets silhouetted against the fires below. One German pilot, Lieutenant Musset of 5/NJG1, accounted for four heavy bombers single-handed; he was flying a Messerschmitt Bf 110, and his observer/radio operator was Corporal Hafner. His combat report makes interesting reading, not least because it reveals how effective the German night-fighter force was at this juncture of the war.

At 2347 hours on 17.8.43 I took off from Berlin on a **Wilde Sau** *operation. From the Berlin area I observed enemy activity to the north. I promptly flew in that direction and positioned myself at a height of 4300 metres over the enemy's target, Peenemünde. Against the glow of the burning target I saw from above numerous enemy aircraft flying over it in close formations of seven or eight.*

I went down and placed myself at 3400 metres behind one enemy formation. At 0142 I attacked one of the enemy with two burst of fire from directly astern, registering good strikes on the port inboard engine, which at once caught fire. E/A (enemy aircraft) tipped over to its left and went down. Enemy counter-fire from rear gunner was ineffective. Owing to an immediate second engagement I could only follow E/A's descent on fire as far as a layer of mist.

I make four claims, as follows:

1. *Attack at 01.45 on a four-engined E/A at 2600 metres from astern and range 30–40 metres. E/A at once burned brightly in both wings and fuselage. I observed it until it crashed in flames at 0147.*

2. *At 0150 I was in position to attack another E/A from slightly above, starboard astern and range 60–70 metres. Strikes were seen in starboard wing, and E/A blew up. I observed burning fragments hit the ground at 0152.*

3. *At 0157 I attacked another four-engined E/A at 1830 metres from 100 metres astern. Burning brightly in both wings and fuselage it went into a vertical dive. After its crash I saw the wreckage burning at 0158. Heavy counter-fire from rear gunner scored hits in both wings of our own aircraft.*

4. *At 0159 I was ready to attack again. E/A took strong evasive action by weaving. While it was in a left-hand turn, however, I got in a burst from port astern and range 40–50 metres, which set the port wing on fire. E/A plunged to the ground burning brightly, and I observed the crash at 0201. Enemy counter-fire from rear gunner was ineffective.*

A few minutes later I attacked another E/A which took violent evasive action by weaving. On the first attack my cannon went out of action owing to burst barrels. I then made three further attacks with MG and observed good strikes on the staboard wing without, however, setting it on fire. Owing to heavy counter-fire from enemy rear gunner I suffered hits in my own port engine. At the same time I came under heavy fire from aircraft on the starboard beam, which wounded radio operator in the left shoulder and set my Me 110's port engine on fire. Thereupon I broke off the action, cut my engine and flew westwards away from the target area. No radio contact with the ground could be established, and ES signals were also unavailing. As I was constantly losing height, at 1800 metres I gave the order to bale out.

As I did so I struck the tail unit with both legs, thereby breaking my right thigh and left shin-bone. After normal landings by parachute my observer and I were taken to the reserve military hospital at Güstrow.

According to the most realistic estimate, the attack set the V2 programme back by two months. It also led to a reappraisal of the programme; two weeks later, the Army High Command informed Dornberger that in future the majority of flight trials, including tests of operational V2s, were to take place at Heidelager, a former SS training camp near Blizna in south-east Poland, between Cracow and Lvov.

Meanwhile, in the first half of 1943, the Russians had gradually been gaining the ascendency on all fronts. The battle for Stalingrad was over, and the German Sixth Army there had been annihiliated. Now, with the coming of the 1943 spring thaw, large-scale operations everywhere came to a virtual standstill, and as they had done a year earlier, both sides took the opportunity to strengthen their forces in preparation for a summer offensive. On the central front, these preparations culminated in the Battle of Kursk in July 1943, which ended in a Russian victory and effectively sealed the fate of Army Group Centre.

At the end of August, supported by 100 air divisions totalling 10,000 aircraft, the whole Soviet battlefront began to roll westwards. Kharkov was recaptured on 23 August, and the German armies, their reserves exhausted, fell back towards the river Dnieper. By mid-September the Soviet Southern and Southwestern fronts had driven the enemy from the Donets basin, and on the 22nd of that month the Dnieper was reached by the 3rd Guards Tank Army. On 6 November the Russians recaptured Kiev after bitter fighting, and Soviet forces crossed the Dnieper at a number of other points. Further north, the Central Front under General Rokossovsky breached the river and reached the Pripet marshes, while the Western Front recaptured Smolensk and drove on towards Vitebsk.

And on the Leningrad front, the Soviet armies were massing for the onslaught that would end the city's misery, and drive the Germans back to the borders of their homeland.

Divide and Conquer

On 12 January 1943, preceded by a massive artillery bombardment, General Govorov's Sixty-Seventh Army and General Meretskov's Second Shock Army launched simultaneous attacks on German forces in the Schlusselberg salient, the farthest point of the German advance on Leningrad. So long as the enemy occupied this salient, the citizens of Leningrad were dependent on the unreliable surface of Lake Ladoga for the final stage of their supply line; but now the Russians advanced inexorably, inflicting heavy losses, and by 18 January they had forced a passage seven miles wide through the salient. While the offensive was still in progress, Soviet engineers began rebuilding the railway line that linked Schlusselberg with Leningrad, a task that included building a bridge over the Neva river, and on 7 February the first train to run into Leningrad since the siege began sixteen months earlier steamed into the city's Vitebsk station to a tumultuous welcome. The siege was not yet lifted, but the turning point in the battle for the city's survival had been reached.

Moreover, it was now possible for the Russians to bring in trainloads of heavy equipment and fresh troops, and duiring the remaining months of 1943 a bridgehead of immense firepower was built up in the Oranienbaum sector, away to the west of Leningrad on the southern bank of the Gulf of Finland. The Soviet intention now was to amass overwhelming superiority in men and equipment before launching the next major offensive, in January 1944, when the forces in the Oranienbaum bridgehead would attack south-eastwards towards Narva and those holding the front east of Leningrad at Volkhov and Novgorod would attack to the south-west towards Luga.

On the Karelian Isthmus, the Finns, bolstered by some German troops, occupied much the same line they had reached in 1941, having never taken part in the direct assault on Leningrad. But Karelia was the scene of bitter and merciless warfare, as this German soldier's account testifies:

Two Finns brought in an Ivan. He was trembling all over, his legs would not support him and he had to be held up under his armpits.

The prisoner was led away and a strange silence reigned for a few minutes. It was suddenly broken by deafening screams, shouts and rifle shots. Hand grenades were thrown, and machine-pistols rattled off bursts of fire. When the noise died away a little we could make out the piercing screams of a man; a man in peril of death. The Finnish lieutenant stood up, stock-still, and listened.

'A friend of ours,' he whispered.

The Russian prisoner had to call out his name. But the Russians demanded the name of an officer whom, so they said, the Finns had taken an hour ago. Lieutenant Nikonen replied that they did not know an officer of that name and that the Finns had not taken any Russian officer.

A German Tiger tank rumbles through a Russian village near Leningrad, 1943. (Bundesarchiv)

Quiet again. Then a scream that did not seem to originate from a human being tore through the wood.

Lieutenant Nikonen's head sank on his chest. 'Is comrade of ours,' he whispered.

Another scream, and another, and another; until it seemed as if the vast dark wood would be ripped to shreds by these terrible screams of agony. The lieutenant covered his eyes with his hand; the Finns stood like statues, their faces turned towards the other side. Now we could hear the Finn sob out words.

'Cut off ears . . .' whispered Nikonen. After a short silence the Finn began again. His head bent low, the Finnish lieutenant said: 'Now nose . . .'

I saw Lieutenant Schleiermacher press his knuckles into his mouth; I was bathed in a cold sweat. A man was being tortured. There were a few more cries, then sobs, whimpering, and then silence. It was ghastly.

Lieutenant Nikonen took off his steel helmet; the other Finns did the same, and so did we. They made the sign of the cross, and in an undertone the Finnish officer said a prayer, in which the men joined softly.

Although I had witnessed terrible scenes in this Karelian wood, I shall never forget this one as long as I live. It was the worst of them all.

What happened next was like a bad dream. The Finns put on their steel helmets, and as one man they rushed forward into the darkness of the wood. We followed, the lieutenant and I, firing our machine-pistols . . .

After taking barely ten steps I was hit in the left shoulder and lost consciousness. That, thank God, was the end of the war in Karelia for me.

At the end of 1943 the troops of the Leningrad Front occupied strong positions along the coast of the Gulf of Finland and to the south-east of Leningrad, while to the south of them were the troops of the Volkhov and Second Baltic Fronts. Opposing them, Army Group North had constructed a strong defensive line some 150 miles in depth. The Russians now had a superiority of two to one over the Germans in infantry and artillery, and were six times stronger in tanks and self-propelled guns. Soviet air power, too, was formidable, with some 1200 aircraft at the disposal of the 13th and 14th Air Armies, the Long-Range Aviation (ADD), the 2nd Guards Fighter Corps and the Baltic Fleet.

The task of the 13th Air Army (General S.D. Rybalchenko) was to support the offensive of the Second Shock Army and the Forty-Second Army from the Leningrad Front, its object to surround and destroy the enemy concentrations in the area of Krasnoye Selo, Ropsha, and Stelna and then join the drive to Kingisepp and Gatchina, while the 14th Air Army (General I.P. Zhuravlev) was to support the Volkhov Front's Fifty-Ninth Army, which was to attack towards Novgorod and then exploit

Aircraft like the Pe-2 light bomber were available to the Russians in huge numbers by 1943, and were extremely effective in the close support role.
(Author's collection)

towards Luga. The object was nothing less than the destruction of the German Eighteenth Army.

The Soviet offensive began on 14 January 1944, troops of the Second Shock Army advancing towards Ropsha in the wake of an artillery barrage. While this barrage was in progress, thirty Il-2s of the 277th Ground-Attack Air Division attacked enemy artillery, although their efforts were jampered by bad weather. Il-2s of this unit, and of the 9th Air Division, were assigned to direct battlefield support, fighter cover being provided by the 275th Fighter Air Division. By the end of the day the Russians had advanced two and a half miles against stubborn resistance, their attack hampered to some extent by bad weather, which curtailed air operations. The Forty-Second Army's offensive opened the next day and was effectively supported by Il-2 assault aircraft of the 9th and 277th Ground-Attack Air Divisions, their attacks being directed from mobile command posts located within the Russian armoured spearheads. Ropsha and Krasnoye Selo were both liberated; in Ropsha, the German communications sytem was seriously disrupted by air attack, an important command centre being completely destroyed.

In parallel with these operations, the Fifty-Ninth Army also went on the offensive on the Volkhov Front. Il-2s of the 281st Ground-Attack Air Division operated on this front, together with units of the 269th Fighter Air Division, the 4th Guards Bomber and the 386th Night Bomber Air Regiments. Many sorties were also flown by units of the Baltic Fleet Aviation, including the 73rd Bomber Air Regiment.

Soviet troops crossed the ice on Lake Ilmen south of Novgorod and took the Germans by surprise, overrunning a defensive strongpoint at Podberezhye and cutting the road between Chudovo and Novgorod. In the course of a week-long battle, the Russian forces opened a breach thirty miles wide by twelve deep, and by 21 January the Soviet line of advance extended from the Gulf of Finland to Lake Ilmen. The blockade of Leningrad, which had cost the lives of a million civilians and 300,000 Russian soldiers, was broken at last.

Within just a few days the Germans were forced to surrender the artillery positions which had been shelling Leningrad for two years and four months. Such was the surprise of the Russian attack that the Germans left eighty-five guns and their ammunition intact, and the Russians lost no time in turning the artillery pieces against their former owners, hastening the pace of their retreat. The retreat continued during the last two weeks of January. The Russians took a thousand prisoners and completely destroyed two German divisions, capturing 265 guns, 159 mortars, thirty tanks, 274 machine guns, and eighteen ammunition depots. The railway junction at Mga was taken, and by 29

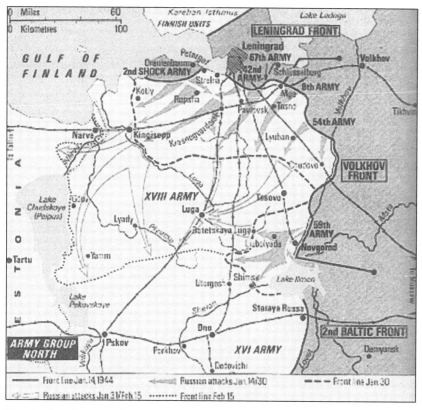

The Soviet offensive of January 1944, that lifted the Leningrad blockade.

January other important railway centres at Chudovo and Lyuban were also under Soviet control. The rail link between Moscow and Leningrad was once more established.

Summing up the Russian offensive of January 1944, the official history of the Soviet Air Force in World War II states:

> *The victory gained by Soviet troops at Leningrad and Novgorod had great military and political significance. During the course of this offensive operation the enemy's northern strategic flank was destroyed, the blockade of Leningrad was broken, the city freed from any danger from artillery fire, the Leningrad and part of the Kalinin districts were liberated, a base was provided for the Red Banner Baltic Fleet, and conditions were created for the liberation of Vyborg and the Soviet Baltic Regions.*

The Baltic Fleet, in fact, had played no small part in the Russian victory. Since 5 November 1943, small craft from Leningrad had been quietly transporting 44,000 troops of the Second Shock Army, plus over 200 tanks, 600 guns, 30,000 tons of supplies, 2400 vehicles and 6000 horses to the Oranienburg bridgehead, while Soviet warships at Kronstadt and on the Neva had fired 24,000 shells in support of the offensive. Naval operations proper, however, did not resume until March, after the thawing of the Baltic ice, when the German destroyers Z25, Z28 and Z39 moved into the Gulf of of Finland to shell Soviet positions near Hungerburg. In April and May, German and Finnish ships laid fresh mine barrages in the approaches to the Gulf of Finland, just as they had done a year earlier, but this time there was a difference; the minelayers came under frequent air attack by Russian fighter-bombers. The Russians now had mastery of the air.

CHAPTER THIRTEEN

The Battle of the Narva Bridgehead

I n February, 1944, the Soviet Volkhov and Leningrad fronts resumed their offensive operations, this time with the objective of driving Army Group North from its positions near Oranienbaum and, ultimately, out of Estonia. In the process, it was hoped that the German Eighteenth Army would be encircled and annihilated.

The main weight of the attack fell on the III (Germania) SS Panzer Corps, led by *Obergruppenführer* Felix Steiner, a man of formidable leadership ability. This international SS Corps had its origins in 1940, when, following Germany's successful campaign in the west, Germany occupied countries whose 'Aryan' populations proved invaluable to the expansion plans of the SS. Danish and Norwegian volunteers formed the Nordland Regiment, while Dutchmen and Flemish Belgians formed the Westland Regiment. These, together with the Germania and the 5th SS Artillery Regiment, combined to form the SS Wiking Division in late 1940. The *Verfügungsdivision* of the SS (literally Support Division, at the disposal of the army and later renamed the Waffen, or armed SS) together with a regiment of the *Totenkopf* (Death's Head) Division was renamed *Das Reich Division*. The *Leibstandarte* Adolf Hitler (Adolf Hitler's Bodyguard) became a brigade, and later a division, and another brigade, *Kampfgruppe Nord*, formed on the Finnish front from *Totenkopf* regiments, became a division in 1942. By 1944 Steiner's SS Corps was made up of many different nationalities, with volunteer units from the Netherlands, Hungary, Romania, Italy, Spain and the Baltic States swelling its ranks.

The Russians quickly broke through the Corps' weak spot, which was held by two infantry divisions composed of *Luftwaffe* personnel, and this

An extremely able and talented commander, Obergruppenführer *Felix Steiner faced impossible odds in the Baltic States.* (Bundesarchiv)

compelled Army Group North to execute a rapid withdrawal to new positions on the Narva river in Estonia. The withdrawal was covered by Steiner's SS Corps, which fought several bitter and bloody engagements as it brought up the rear.

The Narva river provided a natural chokepoint between the northern end of Lake Peipus and the Baltic. The SS Corps set up a defensive line stretching for over seven miles east of the town of Narva, from the village of Lilienbach in the north to Dolgaya Niva in the south. The Corps had barely started digging in when a Soviet armoured attack developed, a strong armoured group penetrating the German line and establishing a foothold on the western bank of the Narva. This was quickly eliminated by four Tiger tanks, which knocked out several T-34s and then supported SS Grenadiers as they dealt with the Russian infantry. Tigers were also in action to the south of Narva, where the defensive line was also penetrated. After a fierce battle, in which troops of the newly-formed Estonian SS Waffen-Grenadier Division played a key part, the Russians were pushed back across the river on 29 February.

General Leonid Govorov, commanding the Leningrad Front, realised that there was little chance of breaching the Narva Line until the German bridgehead on the east bank was eliminated. He therefore ordered a heavy assault in the Lilenbach area, which was defended by men of the 49th (Nederland) SS *Panzergrenadier* Regiment 'De Ruyter' under SS-*Obersturmbannführer* Hans Collani, a Finnish veteran of the Wiking Division. After an artillery duel between the Dutch defenders and the Soviet attackers, the attack disintegrated into fierce hand to hand fighting between the Soviet infantry and the outnumbered troops of Regiment de Ruyter. After several hours of fierce combat, the Russians fell back. De Ruyter had held the line, and Govorov decided to shift the focus of the attack elsewhere. Over the next few weeks, the

SS troops advancing through the ruins of a Russian town. (Bundesarchiv)

Nederland was subjected to almost constant artillery and aerial attacks.

On the night of 6/7 March, 1944, the Soviet Air Force launched a heavy attack on the town of Narva, causing massive damage, and followed it up with an artillery barrage that caused the civilian populace to flee, leaving the rubble to the defenders. During the hours of daylight, a heavy barrage was directed against the Danmark Regiment of the SS Nordland Division, but this was a feint; when the assault came, it fell on the 48th (Nederland) SS *Panzergrenadier* Regiment 'General Seyffardt', in the line to the south of Danmark. Taken by surprise, the Dutchmen were forced out of their positions, but were rallied by their commander, SS-*Standartenführer* Wolfgang Jörchel, who organised a counterattack and destroyed the attacking Russians after intesnse hand-to-hand fighting.

Govorov now switched the focus of his attack back to Lilienbach and Collani's regiment, which was softened up by a heavy barrage before being assaulted by a Soviet infantry force with armoured support. Despite putting up fierce resistance, Collani's men were pushed back. The Russians made a breakthrough, and throwing his reserve armour into the fray, Govorov ordered his men to make for the bridges over the Narva river. The Russian advance was held up by a German armoured counter-attack, but this in turn was halted by accurate Soviet anti-tank fire. Collani ordered his men to leave the Lilienbach position and take up new defensive positions further south.

Soviet air reconnaissance detected the withdrawal, and the retreating Dutchmen were subjected to intense artillery fire and air attack. The De Ruyter suffered heavily, and only the actions of SS-*Untersturmführer*

Watched by soldiers of the SS Norge Regiment, a Panther tank of the Hermann von Salza detachment moves into position. (Bundesarchiv)

Helmut Scholz and his men averted disaster. Scholz's depleted company retook the trenchline and then cut through a Soviet encirclement to rescue SS-*Hauptsturmführer* Karl-Heinz Ertel's II Battalion. For a week, relative peace descended on the front lines, until on 22 March yet another Soviet barrage fell on Collani'stroops. Red Army troops attacked, annihilating the 5th Kompanie and breaking through into the regiment's rear. SS-*Hauptsturmführer* Heinz Frühauf formed an assault group from his headquarters personnel and attacked the Soviet force, which was about 150 strong, destroying it in heavy fighting, before re-forming his men and clearing the regiment's trenches of enemy troops.

After two months of heavy fighting both sides were exhausted, and there was relief when the spring thaw brough a halt to offensive operations for the time being. The Russians kept up constant artillery and air attacks on the enemy lines, however, inflicting further casualties on a German force that was already becoming seriously depleted.

On 23 March, Adolf Hitler directed that Narva was to be designated a fortress city and was to be held at all costs. Because of the thaw there was little activity on the ground in April and May, which gave the Germans some breathing space in which to consolidate their positions, but the respite was not to last for long. The end of May signalled the end of the thaw, and the ground began to dry. Govorov had spent the time reinforcing his southern flank and preparing for an all-out attack against the town of Dolgaya Niva, held by the Danmark Regiment of the SS Nordland Division.

On 7 June, hundreds of Soviet guns opened up all across the seven-mile Narva front. The entire Thirteenth Air Army of the Red Air Force took to the skies with minimal *Luftwaffe* opposition. Special attention was paid by the Russians to the Danmark's positions. As the smoke from the bombardment cleared, the Danes found themselves under attack from masses of Soviet infantry, coming on in human waves. The initial attacks were broken up by SS Nordland's artillery, but the Russians nevertheless reached the Danish positions and fierce fighting developed. The Danes held on grimly over the next four days, but on 12 June the Russians broke through and occupied a key strongpoint, threatening the approaches to the Narva bridges. Only prompt action by SS *Scharführer* Egon Christofferson saved the situation. Counter-attacking with a depleted infantry company, he pushed the Russians back and restored the line, which continued to hold in the face of repeated Soviet assaults.

Although Steiner's SS Corps continued to hold the line, his reservoir of manpower was becoming increasingly depleted. Steiner realised that his men could not hold out for much longer, and that to attempt to do so would be to risk annihilation. He therefore ordered work to begin on a new defensive line, the Tannenberg Line (Tannenbergstellung), located on a series of hills to the west of Narva. Time would be needed to make

During a brief lull in the fighting, men of the 20th (Estland) Waffen SS Division take pleasure in the company of a small companion. (Bundesarchiv)

the new defences ready, and Steiner's corps would have to hold out until then.

And hold out they did. When Govorov ordered an attack against the northern flank of the SS Corps, it was contained by the Estonians of the 20th Waffen Grenadier Division, with timely armoured support. Fresh Soviet attacks against the German bridgehead on the eastern bank were met with fierce resistance from the Danes and Dutchmen. For over a month the bridgehead held against fierce and incessant Soviet attacks. Despite this, the SS Volunteer regiments were now reduced to less than battalion strength, and would not be able to hold out for much longer. News of the successes of Operation *Bagration*, including the destruction of five German divisions near Vitebsk, increased the Russians' morale, and their attacks were stepped up. The Soviet bridgeheads were being reinforced daily, and Steiner knew that an offensive to trap his corps was not far away. On 23 July, despite Hitler's orders to stand or die, Steiner ordered a withdrawal to the Tannenberg Line. The Nederland was tasked with covering the withdrawal, with the General Seyffardt regiment and the artillery battalion the last units to withdraw across the battered Narva bridge.

Govorov was soon aware of Steiner's plans, and on the 24th he launched an all-out attack across the front in an attempt to destroy the withdrawing Germans. The 20th Waffen Grenadier Division was pushed back from the north by a heavy Soviet tank attack, and soon the Tallinn-

Light and extremely manoeuvrable, the Yakovlev Yak-3 was more than a match for the Luftwaffe's *latest fighters.* (ECP Armées)

Narva Rollbahn, the Germans' only line of retreat, was threatened. *Luftflotte* 1 threw every available aircraft into covering the withdrawal, but 137 aircraft were no match for the 800 that could be mustered by the Thirteenth Air Army, equipped now with excellent fighters like the Yakovlev Yak-3 and Yak-9, the Lavochkin La-5 and La-7.

Somehow, the rearguard managed to hold the Russians back while the last of Steiner's men crossed the Narva bridge. But the withdrawal was only accomplished at the expense of the General Seyffardt Regiment, which had been ordered to withdraw by a different route and which now found itself trapped. Subjected to withering attacks from the air and ground, the regiment was utterly destroyed. A handful of Dutch survivors evaded capture and reached the Tannenberg Line a few days later.

On the afternoon of the 24 July, the artillery battalion of the Nederland withdrew across the Narva bridge, which was then blown by sappers from the Nordland's Pioneer Battalion. With the exception of the General Seyffardt, the withdrawal had been a success, and Steiner's men began to dig in on the Tannenberg Line, in preparation for the next Soviet attacks.

The battle of Narva was over. While the Russians could claim a victory, they had been held from their objectives for months by a force a fraction of their size; a force which had now escaped largely intact.

CHAPTER FOURTEEN

The End in Karelia

Throughout 1943, the Finnish Army, encamped fifteen miles to the north of Leningrad and disappointed in their expectation of a short war, had concentrated on transforming the Karelian Isthmus into a powerful fortified region. The defensive system comprised three zones with reinforced concrete strongpoints, the front line fortifications having walls up to eight feet thick and capped with concrete up to ten feet thick. Between seven and fifteen miles farther back, the second defensive line consisted of some 1300 lesser strongpoints. The whole zone was over sixty miles in depth, with the major defensive concentration around Vyborg (Viipuri). Six Finnish divisions were assigned to these defensive positions, supported by 300 aircraft of the Finnish Air Force and some units of *Luftlotte* 1.

It was on the Karelian Isthmus that the weight of the planned Soviet northern offensive in the summer of 1944 was to fall; but this was only part of the great scheme of things.

In April and May 1944 the Russians liberated the Crimea. This was the last major operation before the main Soviet effort of 1944, the objective of which was the destruction of the German Army Group Centre. Centred on Minsk, this Army Group, which was under the command of Field Marshal Walter Model, comprised the Second, Fourth and Ninth Armies and the Third Panzer Army – a total of fifty divisions, with 1000 tanks and 1,200,000 men. For air support, the *Luftwaffe* had managed to scrape together about 1400 combat aircraft.

The destruction of Army Group Centre would not only result in the expulsion of German forces from the Soviet Union; the Army Group was defending what amounted to a broad highway that led into the heart of Central Europe, and if Model's forces were smashed, that highway would be left wide open. In readiness for the offensive, the Russians assembled over two and a half million men on four fronts, stretching in

General Konstantin Rokossovsky pictured in his command post, 1944. (Via J.R. Cavanagh)

a huge shield from north to south. The most northerly of the four was the 1st Baltic Front, which extended from Velikiye Luki on the River Dvina to Vitebsk and was under the command of General I.K. Bagramyan, a redoubtable Armenian who had shown distinguished leadership at the Battle of Orel in the summer of 1943; then came the 3rd Byelorussian Front, lying between Vitebsk and the Dnieper and commanded by General Ivan Chernyakhovsky; this linked up with the 2nd Byelorussian Front under General Matvei Zakharov, whose forces were concentrated on the Dnieper at Mogilev; while the fourth front and the biggest of all, the 1st Byelorussian under General Konstantin 'Steel Teeth' Rokossovsky, stretched from the Dnieper across the Pripet Marshes to Kovel, where its flank was guarded by the Eighth Guards Army under General Vassili Chuikov, the defender of Stalingrad.

To the north of this mighty concentration lay the 2nd and 3rd Baltic Fronts and, finally, the Leningrad Front, whose forces would have the honour of opening the offensive in the north.

The attack by the Leningrad Front against the Finnish positions in Karelia began on 9 June, 1944, and was preceded by very accurate and effective attacks on the Finnish first line of defence by 215 Soviet bombers and 155 ground-attack aircraft, under strong fighter escort. Other attacks were made on railroad communications to the rear, and on known artillery positions, plotted by intensive Russian air reconnaissance. Soviet reconnaissance pilots made 610 sorties prior to the attack, photographing 33,620 square miles of Finnish territory. Mindful of the fact that the *Luftwaffe* and Finnish Air Force were still capabale of carrying out damaging attacks on Russian airfields, the 13th Air Army constructed a network of dummy airstrips, placing 252 dummy aircraft and 176 dummy installations on them.

The ground offensive began with an artillery barrage from a huge concentration of guns, up to 250 per mile. The Twenty-First Army under General D.N. Gussev had been assigned the main assault, which developed over a ten-mile front along the coastal strip and allowed the guns of the Baltic Fleet to lend their support. Writing of these events much later, Finland's Marshal Mannerheim recorded that:

> *June 10th may with reason be described as the black day of our war history. The infantry assault, carried out by three divisions of the Guards against a single Finnish regiment, broke the defence and forced the front in the coastal sector back about six miles. Furious fighting raged at a number of holding lines, but the on-storming massed armour broke their resistance.*
>
> *Because of the enemy's rapid advance, the 10th Division fighting on the coast sector lost most of its artillery. On June 11th, its cut-up units were withdrawn behind the VT (Vammelsuu-Taipale) position to be brought up to strength.*

The Finns made desperate efforts to reinforce their crumbling first line of defence, throwing in reserves, but these were barely in place when they were driven back by a strong Soviet attack that developed north of the Vyborg-Leningrad railway. The Finns fell back on Vyborg, fighting fiercely all the way, but on 17 June the Russians broke through their second line of defence and two days later the third line was also breached, troops of the Twenty-First Army overrunning the well-defended positions at Leipasuo, Summa and Karhula. Meanwhile, troops of the neighbouring Twenty-Third Army cleared the Finns from the southern shores of Lakes Suvanto and Vuoksi.

In the air, resistance stiffened as the *Luftwaffe* moved JG54, now equipped with Focke-Wulf Fw 190s, and the Ju 87s of *Stukageschwader* StG1 to the Vyborg sector. These reinforcements caused some problems for the Russians, as the official history describes:

> *Our aircraft bases became rather distant from the front line as our troops advanced. Because of this the fighters of the 275th Air Division could not give constant support to our troops on the battlefield, while the 2nd Guards Fighter Air Corps was protecting Leningrad and could not be used for ground support. Because of these conditions, fighter aircraft located on advance airfields had to operate at maximum levels. For example, on June 19, Front fighter planes were involved in 24 air battles and shot down 35 enemy aircraft. The next day, there were 28 air battles in which 200 aircraft from both sides participated . . .*

The pace of the Soviet offensive in Karelia was slackening, but on 20 June Russian troops stormed Vyborg and captured it after savage fighting. By the end of June the Finns found themselves roughly on the same line they had occupied at the end of the Winter War of 1939-40, and it was here that the Soviet offensive was halted in the battle of Tali-Ihantala, which lasted from 25 June to 9 July. By this time the Finns, their forces reduced to four depleted divisions, were already suing for peace, having made an initial approach to the Russians on 21 June, but the Russians were demading unconditional surrender, which was unacceptable to the Finnish government.

The battle of Tali-Ihantala was fought in a relatively restricted area between the Gulf of Viipuri and the River Vuoksi. The Russian attack was concentrated in the area east of Vyborg, from the village of Tali north towards Ihantala – the only part of the swampy, forested isthmus that was remotely suitable for armoured operations. However, the Finns had now received a substantial number of German anti-tank weapons, and with these they were able to break the back of the Russian armoured assault. They had also concentrated half their available artillery in the sector.

Finland's President Ryti inspects an artillery position. He would soon give way to Marshal Mannerheim. (Via J.R.Cavanagh)

The heaviest fighting took place during the first two days of July. On the 3rd, the Finns intercepted a radio message indicating that the Soviet 63rd Division and 30th Armoured Brigade were about to launch a heavy attack at 0400. At 0358, 250 Finnish guns opened up a furious barrage on the Soviet assembly area, which was also attacked by forty Stukas and a similar number of Finnish bombers. The schedule of the Russian attack was completely disrupted, and the Finns held on.

By 7 July, there were indications that the Russians were transferring their best units to Estonia in readiness for the forthcoming offensive against Army Group North. Although attacks continued elsewhere along the Finnish front, they were contained without too much difficulty.

The Finns were now exhausted, and more than ready to get out of the war. Marshal Mannerheim had repeatedly reminded the Germans that, in the event of their forces retreating in Estonia, Finland would be forced to make peace, even though it might mean concluding such a peace on very unfavourable terms. A Soviet-occupied Estonia would provide the enemy with a base for amphibious invasions and air attacks against Helsinki and other cities, and would strangle Finnish access to the sea. When the Germans actually began to withdraw, the Finnish desire to end the war increased. Perhaps realizing the validity of this point, initial German reaction to Finland's announcement of ambitions for a separate peace was limited to only verbal opposition. President Ryti resigned, and Finland's military leader and national hero, Marshal Mannerheim, was appointed president by the parliament, accepting responsibility for ending the war.

On 4 September a ceasefire ended military action on the Finnish side. The Soviet Union ended hostilities exactly 24 hours after the Finns, and an armistice was signed between the two nations in Moscow on 19 September, 1944. Finland had to make many unpalatable concessions: the Soviet Union regained the borders of 1940, with the addition of the Petsamo area; the Porkkala Peninsula (adjacent to Finland's capital Helsinki) was leased to the USSR as a naval base for fifty years (but returned in 1956), and transit rights were granted; Finland's army was to demobilise with all speed, and Finland was required to expel all German troops from its territory. As the Germans refused to leave Finland voluntarily, the Finns had no choice but to fight their former allies in a conflict that became known as the Lapland War.

Apart from its military casualties, which were quite high, Finland did not suffer nearly as badly as other belligerent countries in World War Two. Two thousand civilians lost their lives, but only relatively narrow frontier regions bore the brunt of heavy fighting. For nearly three years until June 20, 1944, when Vyborg fell, not one major Finnish town was besieged or occupied. Ultimately, Finland was successful in retaining independence, parliamentary democracy and a market economy. Whatever its political shortcomings, the Finnish leadership had been shrewd enough never to declare war on the Western Allies; and this, together with its persistent refusal to agree to German demands for the deportation of Jews from its territory, was a significant factor in restoring Finland's place in the post-war world.

PART FIVE

The Baltic Operation

CHAPTER FIFTEEN

Breakout

The main Russian offensive against Army Group Centre, named Operation *Bagration* after Prince Peter Bagration, a Russian hero of 1812, opened on 22 June, 1944, the third anniversary of the German invasion of the USSR, the first attacks being directed against the key German strongpoints of Vitebsk, Mogilev, Osha and Bobruisk. For several hours, waves of Soviet bombers subjected these bastions to a merciless pounding, and after the bombers had gone, the Russians moved up their heavy artillery and Katyusha rocket batteries and continued the onslaught for several hours more. In spite of the fearful battering they had received, however, the German defenders were still capable of fighting back hard, as the Soviet infantry discovered when their turn came to move in. Their casualties were terrible; nevertheless, two Soviet armies succeeded in linking up west of Vitebsk on 25 June, inflicting heavy casualties on the 3rd Panzer Army, and the fortress itself fell two days later. The following day Mogilev was also captured, but at such appalling cost to the Russians that the 2nd Byelorussian Front was unable to continue the offensive until strong reinforcements arrived.

The greatest initial success came on the 1st Byelorussian front, where – under the brilliant leadership of General Rokossovsky – the Russians managed to isolate part of the German Ninth Army around Bobruisk. The trapped German forces were then systematically torn to ribbons by the Sixteenth Air Army, and on 29 June they were finally overwhelmed by Rokossovsky's troops. By 13 July, the Soviet High Command had achieved its primary aim: the German Army Group Centre had virtually ceased to exist. The Soviet armies were entering the Baltic States from the east and were preparing to pursue the remnants of Army Group Centre into East Prussia, while the 1st Byelorussian Front was on Polish territory and heading for the Vistula and Warsaw.

In Estonia, *Gruppenführer* Felix Steiner's III SS Corps, its strength

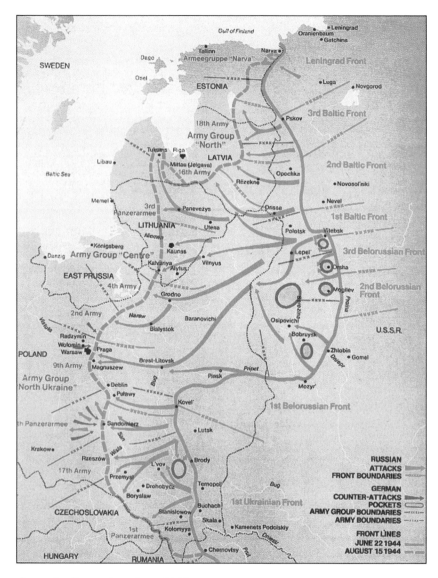

Operation Bagration, *June 1944.*

bolstered by two newly-arrived Belgian SS *Kampfgruppen* – the 5th SS Volunteer Storm Brigade Wallonia and the 6th SS Volunteer Storm Brigade Langemarck – had fallen back to the Tannenberg Line, a far from ideal defensive position consisting of three low hills running from east to west. The eastern hill was known as Orphanage Hill, the central one as Grenadier Hill, and that on the western flank was designated simply Hill 69.9. The SS Langemarck Brigade was assigned to Orphanage Hill, alongside the Norge Regiment of the Nordland Division. The hill was subjected to immediate and heavy Soviet assaults, but the SS men held on with the help of the Wallonia Brigade and elements of the 20th (Estland) *Waffengrenadier* Division.

The position was subjected to further heavy attacks during the following week, but the defenders continued to hold on with the support of the Tiger and Panther tanks of SS *Sturmbannführer* Willi Jähde's 502nd Heavy Armoured Detachment and elements of the Nordland's Hermann

*A German
infantryman digs in.*
(Via J.R. Cavanagh)

The crew of a camouflaged Tiger tank and infantry before the attack.
(Via J.R. Cavanagh)

von Salza Armoured Detachment. Between them, the Tigers and anti-tank guns destroyed 113 Soviet armoured vehicles, including many T-34s and assault guns. During these attacks, Flemish SS-*Unterscharführer* Remi Schrijnen of the Langemarck's anti-tank company singlehandedly destroyed over a dozen Russian tanks while wounded and cut off from the rest of the *Kampfgruppe*. Over a forty-eight hour period, Schrijnen, acting as loader and gunner for his 7.5cm PaK 40 anti-tank gun, personally halted several Soviet tank attacks which otherwise would have encircled the Langemarck and Estland. For his actions, Schrijnen was awarded the Knight's Cross.

Despite the tenacity of the defenders, the Soviet superiority in men, armour and artillery meant that there could only be one outcome, and on 27 July the SS men were forced off Orphanage Hill. Units of the Norge Division counter-attacked the next day but were unable to retake the position, and the defence fell back on Grenadier Hill.

There was to be no respite for the exhausted men of Steiner's corps. Relentless Soviet attacks continued throughout the month of August, and despite inflicting immense casualties on the enemy, the SS units were slowly being worn down. The Nederland was now reduced to the size of a regiment, the Kampfgruppen of the Wallonian and Langemarck each to the strength of a reinforced company. The 20th *Waffengrenadier* Division had virtually lost one of its regiments during the withdrawal and the subsequent fighting, and the Nordland was a shadow of its former self, with the Hermann von Salza Panzer Abt reduced to only two Panthers and a handful of Panzer IVs. All remaining armour available to the defenders was grouped into a *Kampfgruppe, Panzerverband* von Strachwitz, under the command of the *Grossdeutschland* commander and Panzer ace Lieutenant-General Hyazinth Graf Strachwitz von Gross-Zauche und Camminetz. This formation, reinforced by tanks from the *Grossdeutschland*'s Panzer regiment, acted like a fire brigade, seeing heavy fighting along the Narva front and also operating on the southern flank of Army Group North. Strachwitz's *Panzerverband* was disbanded in late July 1944.

Meanwhile, Army Group North found itself in grave danger. Following the success of Operation *Bagration*, the Russians launched a massive assault which effectively isolated the Army Group in a pocket in Kurland (Latvia) and almost succeeded in breaking through to the Gulf of Riga. To counter the threat, *Panzerverband* von Strachwitz was hastily re-formed from elements of the 101st Panzer Brigade (Colonel Meinrad von Lauchert) and the newly-formed SS Panzer Brigade Gross (SS *Sturmbannführer Gross*). Inside the pocket, the remaining tanks and self-propelled guns of the Hermann von Salza and the last of Jähde's Tigers were formed into another battle group.

On 19 August, 1944, both armoured formations launched a simultaneous assault from inside and outside the pocket, and succeeded in restoring contact between Strachwitz and the remnants of the Nordland Division. This operation was

Lieutenant-General Count Hyazinth Strachwitz commanded a Panzergruppe *during the last-ditch fighting in Estonia.* (Via J.R. Cavanagh)

effectively supported by the heavy cruiser *Prinz Eugen*, now with the Baltic Fleet Training Squadron, whose eight-inch shells destroyed forty-eight T-34s assembling in the town square at Tukkum on the Gulf of Riga. Fire support was also provided by the destroyers Z25, Z28, Z35, Z36 and the torpedo boats T23 and T28.

This Russian breakthrough highlighted the vulnerability of Army Group North, and OKH ordered the II Army Corps, then positioned south-west of Lake Peipus in front of the city of Tartu, into Estonia to strengthen the Tannenberg Line defences. Tartu was now virtually defenceless, and on 21 August fifteen Soviet divisions launched an attack towards the city. It was met by von Strachwitz's panzers, which dealt out severe punishment to the enemy before being forced to pull back.

Army Group North was now forced to form scratch battle groups from the surviving remnants of its original fighting forces. One of them was Battle Group Wagner, which comprised elements of the 11th Infantry Division, the SS Wallonia Brigade, the 20th Estonian *Waffengrenadier* Division and various Estonian militia and police formations. The battle group joined the action but was forced back beyond Tartu, settling into defensive positions along the Emajogi river.

On 14 September, 1944, a massive offensive was launched by the Soviet 1st, 2nd and 3rd Baltic Fronts with the twin objectives of capturing Riga and isolating Army Group North in the Kurland area. The German position in Estonia was now no longer tenable, and orders were issued for a total evacuation. After months of holding the line, the exhausted survivors of Steiner's III SS Corps abandoned their Tannenberg Line positions and joined the withdrawal, pursued by the Soviet Second Shock Army. The Estonian capital, Tallinn, was abandoned on 22 September and the Germans concentrated their forces in Kurland. Behind them, they left armed bands of Estonian militia and several companies of the 20th (Estland) *Waffengrenadier* Division, whose men were bent on waging guerrilla warfare against the invading Russians.

These events coincided with the cessation of fighting in Finland, accompanied by the Finnish government's announcement that it was breaking off diplomatic relations with Germany. The *Kriegsmarine* immediately began evacuating 4049 fighting troops and 3336 wounded from Finnish harbours; a great deal of war material had to be destroyed because there was no time to bring it out. A further blow came on 27 September, when Sweden closed her Baltic ports to German shipping.

The loss of the Finnish naval facilities compelled the twelve German U-boats operating in the Baltic to withdraw to Danzig and Gotenhafen, from where they now operated against Finnish shipping in the Gulf of Bothnia. Submarine U479 was lost in a minefield on 12 December 1944, and U679 was depth-charged and sunk by Finnish patrol boats on 9 January 1945.

In the last six months of 1944, the German seaports in the southern Baltic were subjected to increasing attacks by RAF Bomber Command. Although RAF bombers had been attacking distant targets such as Stettin since late 1940, such attacks were made by individual aircraft and were of little significance, and it was not until the attack on Lübeck in March 1942 that Bomber Command showed that it had the capability to hit Baltic targets hard.

The Command's bombing accuracy improved considerably with the intruduction of new navigational aids such as H2S, a radar device that transmitted pulse signals to earth and received back the echoes, which formed a display on a cathode-ray tube. This display consisted of a series of light spots of varying brilliance, which formed a picture of the terrain over which the aircraft was flying. It was particularly effective against coastal targets, which could be readily identified, as the citizens of Stettin discovered on the night of 20/21 April, 1943.

On that night, 339 heavy bombers took off from their bases in eastern England and flew more than 600 miles to attack Stettin. Visibility was good and the Pathfinder target marking excellent. Twenty-four fires were still burning when a photo-reconnaissance Mosquito flew over Stettin a day and a half later. About 100 acres in the centre of the town were completely devastated; much of this area comprised industrial buildings. The civilian death toll was 586. The RAF lost thirteen Lancasters, seven Halifaxes and a Stirling.

Stettin was attacked again on the night of 5/6 January 1944, by 348 Lancasters and ten Halifaxes. The attack began accurately, but later phases of the bombing drifted to the west. The raid caused substantial damage, sinking eight ships in the harbour, and killed 244 people. Sixteen bombers were shot down. A further damaging attack was carried out by 461 Lancasters on 16/17 August, when over 1500 houses and 29 industrial premises were destroyed and as many again badly damaged. Five ships totalling 5000 tons were sunk in the harbour and eight more seriously damaged. The death toll was 1150, with a further 1654 people injured.

On 29/30 August Bomber Command carried out a two-pronged operation against targets on the Baltic, Stettin was hit again, this time by 400 Lancasters, in a successful attack that destroyed parts of the town which had escaped damage in earlier raids. A ship of 2000 tons was sunk in the harbour and seven others damaged. Again, over a thousand people lost their lives and a similar number were injured. On the same night, 189 Lancasters, operating at extreme range, attacked Königsberg. Because of the extreme range only 480 tons of bombs could be carried, but severe damage was caused around the four separate aiming points that had been selected. Bomber Command estimated that 41 per cent of all the housing and 20 per cent of all the industry in Königsberg had been destroyed. This success was achieved despite the fact that the attack was delayed for twenty minutes by low cloud. Fighter opposition over the target was intense, and fifteen Lancasters were shot down.

CHAPTER SIXTEEN

The Russian Avalanche

On 6 October, 1944, Soviet forces broke through to the Baltic coast between Libau and Memel, completely isolating the remnants of Army Group North in the Kurland pocket. The Russians' efforts to consolidate and launch a rapid attack on the pocket were to some extent frustrated by the gunfire of the heavy cruisers *Prinz Eugen* and *Lützow*, together with the destroyers Z25, Z35 and Z36, which shelled Soviet assembly areas near Memel. Anti-submarine and anti-aircraft defence for this small but effective naval task force was provided by the 3rd Torpedo-Boat Flotilla, consisting of the T21, T13, T16 and T20, which succeeded in beating off a number of Soviet air attacks.

The main effort of what remained of Army Group North was now concentrated on defending the town of Libau, which would be the principal embarkation port should the evacuation order be issued. The harbour was subjected to a heavy Soviet air attack on 14 December, in which three transport vessels were sunk and several more damaged. Four days later, 236 Lancasters of RAF Bomber Command attacked the harbour of Gotenhafen (Gdynia), dropping 824 tons of bombs and sinking four freighters and a tanker in addition to a U-boat depot ship, the torpedo boat T10, a target vessel and a training ship. The latter was none other than the *Schleswig-Holstein*, which had been undergoing a refit. She was officially decommissioned on 25 January, 1945, and later broken up where she lay.

So far, the German forces in Kurland had been supplied from the ports on the Gulf of Danzig and the western Baltic, the supply ships unloading at Libau and Windau (Ventspils). The transports were escorted by minesweepers. Over the weeks that followed, eight of the thirty-five divisions trapped in the Kurland pocket were successfully evacuated to East Prussia and Pomerania, several German steamers being sunk by air and submarine attack. The remainder of the forces in Kurland were destined to remain where they were until the final surrender, bypassed by the Russians.

On 15 January, 1945, Army Group North was renamed Army Group Kurland on the orders of Hitler, and Army Group Centre was redesignated Army Group North. Germany now had to face the end with all her allies gone except Hungary. The last six months of fighting in 1944 alone had cost her 840,000 dead and missing in the east, and a further 393,000 in the west. Her air power was so weakened that in the east the *Luftwaffe* could muster only 1900 aircraft; the Russians had 15,500. Thirteen air armies provided cover for 6,800,000 men organised into fifty-five armies, each of nine infantry divisions plus artillery, and six tank armies, each of two tank and one mechanised corps.

For the assault on East Prussia, the Russians had assembled 1,700,000 men, supported by over 25,000 guns and mortars, 3900 tanks and self-propelled guns and some 3000 aircraft. The Germans had 8200 guns, 700 tanks and 775 aircraft. The Germans had constructed a powerful defensive network in East Prussia, with no fewer than seven defensive lines, strengthened with concrete pillboxes, dragon's teeth and other permanent fortifications, and six fortified regions, each based on a key strategic town.

The 3rd Byelorussian Front, supported by the 1st and 3rd Air Armies, began its offensive into East Prussia on 13 January 1945, its objective being to pin down large numbers of German forces between the Masurian Lakes, a significant obstacle, and the Baltic coast. On the following day the 2nd Byelorussian Front also attacked on the axis Marienburg-Elbing, supported by the 4th Air Army. On 17 January Warsaw was liberated by Soviet and Polish forces, advancing from the Vistula and supported by the 16th Air Army. In the week that followed, Soviet forces reached the riverr Oder. As the rapid advance caused problems for the air support units, thirty-two airfields were built and fifteen restored to operational condition between 26 January and 7 February. In addition, aircraft of the 15th Fighter Air Regiment and 9th Guards Fighter Air Division began operations from stretches of Autobahn. In the twenty days of the Vistula-Oder campaign, the 2nd and 16th Air Armies flew more than 54,000 sorties, claiming the destrruction of 908 enemy aircraft. *Luftwaffe* resistance in East Prussia was weaker; the focus here was on ground-attack operations as Soviet forces overcame the heavily-fortified towns and other strongpoints.

Meanwhile, Admiral Oscar Kummetz, former commander of the German heavy cruiser squadron in Arctic waters and now in charge of the German Naval High Command East, had been putting the finishing touches to the planning for what was to become the greatest naval evacuation in history. Kummetz and his staff now faced the formidable task of evacuating huge numbers of German troops and civilians from Kurland and the Gulf of Danzig, and for this purpose they had assembled a number of large passenger ships which had been employed as accommodation vessels at Pillau, Gotehafen and Danzig. The principal vessels were the *Cap Arkona* (27,561 tons), *Robert Ley* (27,288 tons), *Wilhelm Gustloff* (25,484 tons), *Hamburg* (22,117 tons), *Hansa* (21,131 tons), and *Deutschland* (21,046 tons).

Ships of between 10,000 and 20,000 tons displacement included the *Potsdam, Pretoria, Berlin, General Steuben, Monte Rosa, Antonio Delfino*, and *Winrich von Kniprode*. There were also twenty-five freighters displacing between 5000 and 10,000 tons, and many other lesser ships. Auxiliary warships and escort vessels were also pressed into service.

Apart from the ever-present threat of air attack, two factors conspired to disrupt the evacuation. The first was a vigorous air mining campaign which was conducted by the Royal Air Force in the south-western Baltic; the second was a renewed phase of operations by Soviet submarines following the truce with Finland on 4 September 1944, when the Finns were obliged to sweep a path through the defences close to the Finnish coastline. Navigating with the aid of Finnish naval officers, fifteen boats made their way into the Baltic, armed with mines and torpedoes, and succeded in sinking a score of ships, including the submarine U479, which on 12 December was destroyed in a mine barrage laid by the submarine *Lembit.*

On 25 January 1945 the first evacuation ships sailed from Pillau, carrying 7100 refugees to safety in the west. By 28 January 62,000 refugees had been evacuated. Also evacuated, on the light cruiser *Emden*, was the sarcophagus of President Paul von Hindenburg and that of his wife, which had been buried at the Tannenberg Memorial in East Prussia; the monument itself was blown up. The coffins of Hindenburg and his wife were taken to Marbug an der Lahn in Hesse, where they were hidden in an abandoned salt mine. They were discovered by US troops on 27 April 1945 and re-interred in the Elisabeth Church, Marburg.

Meanwhile, the Soviet Thirty-Ninth and Forty-Third Armies had advanced into the western part of the Samland Peninsula between Königsberg and Cranz, severing land communications between Pillau and Königsberg. XXVII Corps launched an attack south-west from the Cranz bridgehead in an attempt to restore contact, this being supported by the German Navy's Task Force 2 under Vice-Admiral Thiele. The naval task force comprised the heavy cruiser *Prinz Eugen*, the destroyers Z25 and *Paul Jacobi*, and the torpedo boats T23 and T33, which shelled targets ahead of the German advance on 29 and 30 January. Other vessels, operating in the Königsberg Sea Canal, shelled Soviet armour. Later, the heavy cruisers *Lützow* and *Admiral Scheer*, together with the destroyers, lent invaluable fire support to the German Third Panzer Army, counter-attacking from the Fischhausen area.

On 30 January 1945, the evacuation fleet suffered its first major disaster. Early that morning, the 25,484-ton passenger liner *Wilhelm Gustloff* left Gotenhafen, accompanied by another liner, the *Hansa*, and two torpedo boats. The *Hansa* and one torpedo boat developed problems and could not continue, leaving the *Gustloff* with only one torpedo boat as escort. The ship had four senior officers on board and an argument broke out about whether or not to light the red and green navigation lights to avoid a potential collision with an oncoming minesweeper convoy. Captain Peterson, in command, reluctantly agreed to activate the lights, and the ship was subsequently sighted by the Soviet submarine S-13 (Captain Third Class Marinesko), on patrol in the area of the Stolpe Bank. The Gustloff was torpedoed 20 miles offshore, somewhere between Neustadt (present day *Wladyslawowo*) in West Prussia and Leba. Three torpedoes hit the liner, which sank within seventy minutes in 150 feet of water. One account claimed that 400 members of the Women's Auxiliary of the German Navy were killed after the second torpedo hit under the empty swimming pool in which they were sitting. The panic that followed the torpedo hits resulted in more deaths, as many of the refugees ignored orders to allow women and children to disembark first. Many were trampled in a rush for lifeboats and life jackets. Some equipment was lost as a result of the panic. The water temperature in the Baltic Sea at that time of year is usually around 4°C; however, this was a particularly cold day with an air temperature of –10 to –18° with ice floes covering the surface.

At the time of the attack, there were 7956 registered refugees on board the *Gustloff*, but it is estimated that about 2000 more joined the vessel at the last mimute before she sailed, and several hundred refugees from Reval came on board while she was at sea. Together with the crew, the total number must have been well over 10,000, of which only 1239 were saved by torpedo boats and minesweepers. The heavy cruiser *Admiral Hipper*, which was evacuating 1500 wounded soldiers, also came up to help with the rescue effort, but had to withdraw to the west because of the submarine threat.

On the following day the L-3 (Captain Third Class Konovalov) made two abortive attempts to sink the fully laden *Cap Arkona*, but on 10 February the S-13, still cruising in the area of the Stolpe Bank, sank the 14,660-ton liner *General Steuben* with one torpedo. The escort vessels

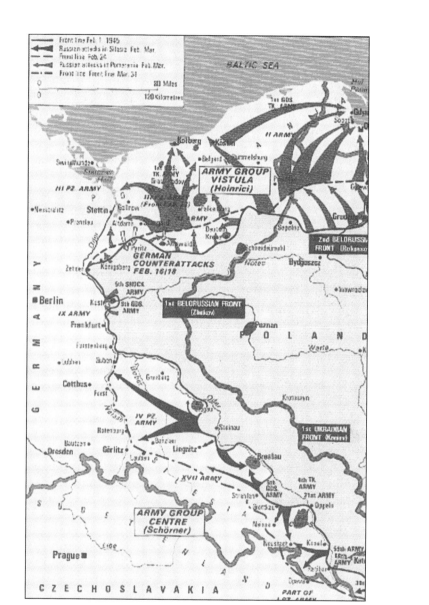

The Soviet Offensive into West Prussia, February 1945.

T196 and TF10 managed to pluck only 300 passengers from the freezing water, the survivors of more than 3000.

For the German people, the first week of February, 1945, was the grimmest of the war. The coming months would bring despair and more destruction – and, in the east, rape and atrocity – but not another shock equal to the sudden appearance of the Russians on the Oder river. Three weeks earlier the front had still been deep in Poland and nowhere on German soil. Now Upper Silesia was lost; in East Prussia a German army group was being cut to pieces; Berlin, West Prussia and Pomerania were being defended by a newly-created formation, little more than a skeleton army, called Army Group Vistula under Heinrich Himmler, who as a military commander was utterly incompetent; and the defence on the Oder was having to be entrusted to armies that had already been defeated on the Vistula and chased across the breadth of Poland. The promises of the 'wonder weapons' that would miraculously turn the tide in Germany's failure were seen as hollow and meaningless. All that remained was twilight, descending with terrifying speed into darkness.

On the left of the Russian advance, Marshal Koniev's 1st Ukrainian Front launched an offensive from the Oder on 8 February and covered the sixty miles to the Neisse river in a fortnight. To German intelligence, it seemed clear that the Soviet drive westwards would continue, and there was practically nothing to stop it. Then, suddenly, the Germans detected a change in the Russians' plans.

On 24 February, Marshal Rokossovsky's 2nd Byelorussian Front, on the right of Marshal Zhukov's 1st Byelorussian Front and facing north into West Prussia, suddenly launched a series of heavy probing attacks. By the end of the first day Rokossovsky's troops had found a weak spot, and by the end of the second they had covered nearly half the distance to the Baltic coast. In Koniev's sector there were also unexpected troop movements, the 4th Tank Army swinging towards northen Czechoslovakia. It seemed clear that the Russians intended to tidy up their flanks before launching their major offensive towards Berlin, especially as Zhukov's forces, which would spearhead any such assault, showed no sign of movement.

Beginning on 24 February, in order to assemble a strong force for the defence of the Samland Peninsula, the German XXVIII Corps was transferred over the ice from the Memel bridgehead to the Kurische Nehrung, the long strip of land linking Memel with Samland. A substantial number of refugees and wounded were also evacuated.

On 28 February, the Germans captured a Russian map which indicated that Rokossovsky was aiming for the Baltic coast east of Köslin with the intention of driving a wedge between III Panzer and Second Armies.

The Luftwaffe *made desperate attempts to destroy the Oder bridges, using both conventional bombs and missiles, in a bid to hold up the Soviet advance. These are* Luftwaffe *damage assessment photographs.* (Bundesarchiv)

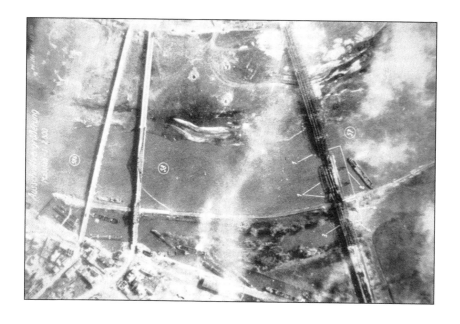

Both these formations, understrength, lacking fuel and artillery ammunition, could do nothing to stop him, and on 1 March the 3rd Guards
Tank Corps reached the coast, severing the road and railway that were
the main lines of communication with Second Army, Danzig and
Gotenhafen.

Then came the unpleasant surprise. On the day that Rokossovsky's
troops reached the Baltic coast, Zhukov sudddenly attacked north. Both
of his tank armies and a shock army smashed through III Panzer Army's
centre, 1st Guards Tank Army racing due north to Kolberg and and 2nd
Guards Tank Army turning north-west towards the mouth of the Oder.
Within four days 1st Guards Tank Army had established a foothold on
the coast, enveloping Kolberg to join its right flank with Rokossovsky's
left. In his book 'Battle for Berlin', Earl F. Ziemke observed that:

> *The envelopment of Kolberg brought a peculiar small embarrassment to
> the Germans. In February Goebbels' Propaganda Ministry had released a
> film entitled Kolberg, a rare colour epic – the most lavish ever made in
> Germany, depicting Gneisenau's defence of the city against the French in
> 1807. Goebbels' epic, in the end, however, escaped also becoming a classic
> propaganda blunder. The old city on the Baltic, which had surrendered
> only one of the three times the Russians besieged it in the Seven Years'
> War and had later stood off Napoleon's troops, though lost at least did not
> surrender in the Second World War. The garrison held out until 18
> March. By then 80,000 inhabitants and refugees had been evacuated by
> sea, and the last few hundred soldiers escaped aboard a destroyer.*

By late February, about a quarter of the German strength on the Eastern
Front, around 560,000 men was bottled up in Kurland and East Prussia.
On 5 March Marshal Zhukov assigned the Fifth Tank Army to
Rokossovsky , who sent it on a drive towards the Bay of Danzig.
Encountering fierce resistance, it would take it a month to reach its
objective.

On 7 March, the 2nd Byelorussian Front attacked from the Köslin-
Vistula line near Marienwerder towards Danzig and Gotenhafen. The
German Second Army was driven back to the line Rixhöft-Neustadt-
Karthaus, where it was able to stabilise its front, albeit only temporarily,
with naval gunfire support, thereby gaining valuable time in which to
evacuate more refugees. From 10 March the *Prinz Eugen* lent fire support
to the operation, and on the 15th she was joined by the old battleship
Schlesien, the gunboats *Soemba*, *Joost* and *Ostsee* and the gunnery training
vessel *Drache*. The *Schlesien* had to be withdrawn on 21 March, leaking at
the seams from the percussion of her guns and lacking ammunition, but

two days later her place was taken by the heavy cruiser *Lützow*, supported by the destroyers Z31 And Z34. So desperate were the Germans for artillery support that the light cruiser *Leipzig*, which had been badly damaged in October 1944 in a collision with the *Prinz Eugen*, was hurriedly made seaworthy again and sent into action.

The evacuation operations from Gotenhafen, Danzig and the Hela Peninsula were now coming under constant air attack by the Soviet Naval Aviation, principally the 9th Ground Attack Division (Lieutenant-Colonel Slepenko) and the 8th Mining and Torpedo Division (Colonel Kurochkin). A formidable AA defence was put up by destroyers, torpedo boats, minesweepers and auxiliary vessels to protect the transports, but inevitably some of the Sturmoviks broke through, and on 12 March they sank the 1761-ton freighter *Gerrit Fritzen*, the minesweeper M3137 and the submarine-chaster UJ303.

Sixteen-year-old Hans Gliewe, fleeing with his mother and younger brother, experienced the horrors of the journey to Danzig, with thousands of others who were desperate to be evacuated.

Next day we spent in the broken trolley cars that were lined up in one place. There were many refugees there. Most of us had not eaten properly for days. Some woman pulled out a cold boiled potato, and everybody envied her. The farmers on the wagons were better off. And the people of Danzig had food, too. But we came from a different section and the shops didn't want to sell to us on our ration tickets. Two little boys fought over a piece of bread.

. . . In the evening we got into the railway station and somehow found a place on a train going north to Oliva. In Oliva we found a house that was deserted. But we were awakened before morning. Russian artillery was shooting away, and from the road we heard the tramping of soldiers and of the many people who were fleeing south into Danzig. When it got light and I saw such a lot of soldiers, I thought the Russians simply couldn't get through. But the soldiers with whom I spoke just sneered and asked me how I expected to stop the Russian tanks – they had beautiful field guns, to be sure, but no ammunition . . . They said the Russians were only a mile and a half away. We were so frightened!

We stood in the cellar door, not knowing what to do. Other refugees came along, dragging their feet.

Then a soldier came by with a truck; he said he was driving to Neufahrwasser and would take us along. So we went. It was getting warmer and the streets were mud. Trucks blocked the road all the way. In one place, soldiers were digging trenches right next to the road. We saw many of the search commandos of the military police and the SS leading away soldiers they had arrested. And this constant flow of ragged people rushing past. I'll never forget it – sometimes one of those faces comes back to me in a dream.

We drove across the airport; there was nothing but a few shot-up machines. Russian planes came over several times but they did not shoot. Then we got to the port. There were no ships. People said that all the Navy evacuation ships were now sailing from Gdynia. The sea looked grey . . . So we went to the camp. We opened the door of one of the wooden barracks. A cloud of stench came to meet us. Hundreds of people sat in there, crowded together on filthy straw piles . . . Next to us sat a woman whose child had just gone down with dysentery. Next morning it lay there, so little and pale.

An Italian prisoner of war who worked on the piers told us that a small ship from Königsberg had arrived and was docking a little farther up the coast. The woman next to us went to take the ferry and go over there. She left the child behind with us and promised to come back and fetch us. She kept her word, too. When she came back she told us that she had met an acquaintance from Königsberg who for five hundred marks and her ring had promised to smuggle her and her child on the ship. He could do nothing for us, but she would not forget us. And she did not forget us. We ran away from the barracks and paid an Italian to row us over to the dock where the ship was. He looked at us sadly, and said in his poor German he would like to go home, too. On the dock we waited near the ship, and finally our 'neighbour' from the barracks – she made out we were her real neighbours – persuaded her acquaintance to smuggle us aboard, too.

Most of those on the ship were from Königsberg. Some of them had gone ashore and were now coming back. We walked along with them as if we belonged. Then we hid in the cold, draughty hold of the ship. We huddled close together, but still we were terribly cold. But we did not dare to move, let alone get up, for fear they would recognise us as stowaways.

The night went by. The rumble of artillery over Danzig grew very loud. A man who had been up on deck said the sky was all red with the fires. We were so happy and grateful that we could lie in the draughty hold of the ship. But we were shaking with fear that we would be found out and put ashore. Then the ship pulled out, and we breathed again.

Despite the shipping losses caused by Soviet air attack and mines, the German transports evacuated huge numbers of people to the west. On 23 March, for example, the *Deutschland* sailed from Gotenhafen with 11,145 people on board, and five days later she took off another 11,295, while the liner Potsdam rescued over 9000 in one uplift.

On 27 March, the non-operational hulk of the battlecruiser *Gneisenau* was sunk as a blockship in Gotenhafen harbour. Damaged by RAF bombs at Kiel shortly after escaping from Brest in February 1942, she had been decommissioned in July that year, her gun turrets removed and used for coastal defence. All repair work on her had been suspended in 1943, and she had been towed to Gotenhafen, her final resting place.

Gotenhafen fell to the Russians on 28 March and Danzig two days later. On the night of 4/5 April, 8000 troops of VII Panzer Corps and about 30,000 refugees were evacuated from the Oxhöfter bridgehead and brought to Hela in 25 naval trawlers, 27 ferry barges, five heavy auxiliary gunboats and five other vessels in an operation dubbed 'Walpurgisnacht'. These and subsequent operations were covered by the heavy cruiser Lützow, accompanied by a number of destroyers and torpedo boats, until 8 April, when the Lützow and two of the destroyers had to be withdrawn because of shortage of fuel and ammunition.

Between 21 March and 10 April 1945, 157,270 wounded were evacuated from the Hela Peninsula, while in April 264,887 refugees were taken by an armada of small craft from the ports that still remained unoccupied in the Gulf of Danzig, Pillau, Kahlberg, Schiewenhorst and Oxhöft. Many of the refugees had to pay for the privilege of escaping the Russians; the

A 12,000lb 'Tallboy' bomb exploding on a German port installation. The Tallboy could penetrate U-boat pens, and was also used to sink the battleship Tirpitz. (IWM)

civilian owners of some craft charged up to 1000 Reichsmarks per person. The refugees who were fleeced in this way had the last laugh, for the Reichsmarks would soon be worthless.

Soviet air activity was on the increase, and with the *Luftwaffe* incapable of intervening the only defence was provided by the anti-aircraft guns of the warships covering the embarkations. After several of these had to be withdrawn, losses among the embarkation vessels mounted. In the week from 7 to 14 April, Soviet aircraft sank the transport *Flensburg* (5450 tons), the fleet supply ship *Franken* (10,850 tons), the repair ship *Hans Albrecht Wedel*, the submarine chasers UJ301 and UJ1102, the hospital ship *Posen*, two minesweepers and the transports *Albert Jensen, Moltkefels, Wiegand* and *Karlsruhe*, all of over 5000 tons.

On 9 April, the number of German warships that might have been made available for operations in the Baltic was further reduced when RAF Bomber Command capsized the heavy cruiser *Admiral Scheer* –

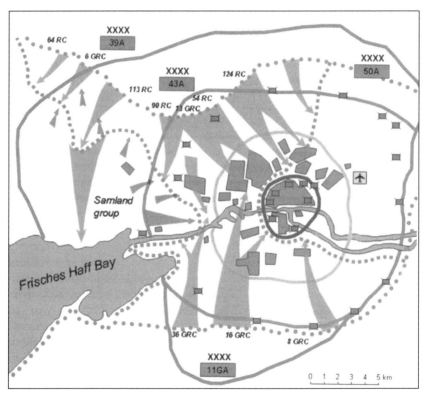

The Battle of Königsberg, April 1945.

which had been the objective of the very first attack carried out by the RAF in the Second World War, on 4 September 1939 – with a 12,000lb 'Tallboy' bomb at Kiel. Two more warships, the cruisers *Admiral Hipper* and *Emden*, were so severely damaged in the same attack that they were unfit for further use.

By now, the Soviet advance had rolled over and past East Prussia, and almost all of its population had trekked out across the sand spits that fringed the Bay of Danzig; but East Prussia's capital, Königsberg, still held out. The 1st Baltic Front and 3rd Byelorussian Front had tried to take the city in February, but had been frustrated by the German Fourth Army's counter-attack from the Samland Peninsula, which had opened a corridor to the city.

Now, in April, the Fourth Army had ceased to exist as a coherent fighting force and Marshal Aleksandr Vasilevsky, commanding the 3rd Byelorussian Front, was ready to try again. Four armies were deployed around Königsberg; inside the fortress, the commandant, General Otto Lasch, had five full-strength divisions, a total of 130,000 men.

The German defensive position was impressive. They still held a narrow land connection to the adjacent German pocket on the Samland peninsula, and this desperately defended corridor would have to be severed as a preliminary to the assault on the city. The German troops on the peninsula, the so-called Samland group, could be expected to stage counter-attacks to prevent this from happening.

Three concentric rings of fortifications surrounded the city: the outer ring of defences reinforced by twelve forts outside the town, the middle ring in the outskirts and the inner city, a single fortress of anti-tank defences, barricades and landmines, supported by several other strong-points. Vasilevsky knew that any infantry assault would have to be preceded by a thorough softening-up of each line of defence, using all available artillery and tactical air power. On 2 April, he therefore ordered a massive artillery bombardment that lasted four days.

In the wake of this, the air attacks began, as the official history describes.

On April 7, from 10.00 am to 1.30pm, 246 Tu-2s and Pe-2s delivered three bombing raids on the fortifications around Königsberg. After this attack by the Front aircraft, 516 18th Air Army bombers made a mass raid during daylight hours. These effective air strikes helped our troops as they quickly drove into the defences of the fortress. The next day, 456 of our bombers hit reserves west of Königsberg.

These mass daytime raids by the 18th Air Army were made possible by our complete control of the air. On April 7, 124 fighters were assigned to escort the bombers. In addition, at the time of the raid, 108 fighter planes patrolled at different altitudes over the city to prevent any enemy fighters from approaching the areas where our bombers were active. Twenty minutes before the bombers arrived, ground-attack planes and bombers struck at the two largest enemy airfields to suppress his fighter units. As a result, the 18th Air Army struck a serious blow at the enemy without losing any planes.

Ground attack planes and fighters, as they supported our advancing troops, destroyed his men and artillery on the battlefield. In addition to destroying the fortifications in Königsberg, the air force attacked enemy troops as they were being shifted from the Samland Peninsula. On April 7, the 1st and 3rd Air Armies' ground-attack planes struck at enemy troops in the forests west of Königsberg. These air operations disrupted an enemy counter-attack planned to break the blockade of the Königsberg garrison.

Because of coordinated ground and air force efforts, the enemy ceased his resistance and on 10 April the Königsberg garrison capitulated. During the four days of the operation the air force flew 14,090 sorties and dropped 4440 tons of bombs on the enemy. Its mass attacks significantly accelerated the enemy's surrender. This was indicated by the captured fascist generals. The German commander of Königsberg, General Lasch, said: 'Air power played a very important role in the capture of Königsberg – the troops were tormented, driven to the ground, pursued into their bunkers.'

It was a fair assessment. And with Königsberg gone, the way was now clear for the Soviet armies to redeploy for the final offensive that would take them on to Berlin.

An excellent tactical bomber, the Tupolev Tu-2 was one of the principal types used to reduce Königsberg to rubble.
(Author's collection)

CHAPTER SEVENTEEN

Baltic Storm

On 15 April 1945, the 3rd Byelorussian front, attacking west-wards, broke through the Samland defences, with the immediate consequence that some 70,000 refugees were left trapped in Pillau. Some managed to struggle to safety along the Frische Nehrung, while others were evacuated by sea. During these operations, three freighters, two of them over 5000 tons, were sunk by air attack. To lend fire support, the shrinking Kriegsmarine scraped together every vessel capable of firing a gun; they comprised five heavy auxiliary gunboats and the gunnery training ship *Drache*. The latter was sunk in an air attack on 18 April.

On 24/25 April, the last night of the evacuation of Pillau, naval ferry barges lifted off 19,200 troops and refugees, bringing the total evacuated from this one spot since 21 January to nearly half a million.

The evacuation focused on the Hela Peninsula, the narrow spit of land jutting out into the Bay of Danzig on its western extremity. On 16 April, a convoy of eight ships leaving Hela came under heavy air attack, the repair ship *Boelcke* being sunk, and during the night the submarine L-3 (Captain Third Class Konovalov) torpedoed and sank the 5230-ton trans-port *Goya*. Only 165 of the 6385 people on board were rescued. On this day, the dwindling assets of the *Kriegsmarine* suffered yet another blow when eighteen Lancasters of No 617 Squadron RAF flew to Swinemünde to attack the heavy cruiser *Lützow*. The bombers attacked through heavy flak; one Lancaster was shot down (the squadron's last loss of the war) and all but two of the others were damaged. Fifteen aircraft bombed the target with 12,000lb 'Tallboy' or 1000lb bombs; the effects of one near-miss by a Tallboy tore a large hole in the bottom of the *Lützow* and she sank in shallow water as her crew tried to beach her.

Further air attacks on the evacuation convoys on 19 and 20 April resulted in the loss of the 5897-ton steamer *Altengamme* and some smaller vessels, and on the 25th the 2435-ton *Emily Sauber* was sunk by Soviet torpedo boats operating out of the newly-captured harbour of Neufahrwasser, Danzig. On 20 April the liner *Eberhard Essberger* sailed from Hela with 6200 refugees, and the following day the *Lappland* sailed for the west with 7700. On 28 April seven steamers evacuated 24,000 refugees were embarked, bringing the total for April to 387,000.

On 30 April, with Soviet troops in the heart of Berlin, Adolf Hitler committed suicide. On the following day the Soviet Second Shock Army, having pushed across the lower Oder, reached the ancient Hanseatic town of Stralsund in western Pomerania, while the Nineteenth Army advanced on Swinemünde. On 2 May, the old battleship *Schlesien*, fighting to the last, was sent to the Greifswalder Bodden – the coastal waters of the southern Baltic off Peenemünde between Rügen and Usedom Islands – to protect the Wolgast Bridge, across which refugees and troops were streaming over the Peene river. As she approached her station, she struck a mine and was towed back to Swinemünde, where she was beached. Two days later she was blown up, together with the adjacent *Lützow*.

Meanwhile, the British Second Army, having crossed the Rhine in March, had pushed on across the North German plain towards the northern German ports, reaching the Elbe on 19 April, and on 2 May, the day on which fighting ceased in Berlin, forward units of the British 6th Airborne Division joined up with advancing troops of the Soviet 70th Army at Wismar, on the Baltic. Supporting the British advance were the ground attack squadrons of the RAF Second Tactical Air Force, equipped mainly with the Hawker Typhoon.

A Hawker Typhoon fighter-bomber of No. 184 Squadron RAF Second Tactical Air Force. (Wing Commander Jack Rose)

On the afternoon of 3 May, 1945, the Second Tactical Air Force unleashed its Typhoon squadrons against enemy shipping in Lübeck Bay, where several large vessels had been sighted by air reconnaissance. The four squadrons of No 123 Wing, operating were briefed to carry out the mission. Nos 184, 263 and 198 Squadrons were armed with cannon and rockets, while No 197 Squadron carried cannon and bombs. It was this squadron that carried out the first attack, on what the pilots described as a 'two-funnel cargo liner of 10,000 tons with steam up in Lübeck Bay'. She was in fact the passenger liner *Deutschland*, which was in the process of being fitted out as a hospital ship. The Typhoon pilots had no means of knowing this, because the ship carried only one small Red Cross marking, painted on one side of a funnel. At the time of the attack the *Deutschland* carried only eighty crew members and a small medical team of twenty-six. The ship was hit by four rockets, one of which failed to explode. Another started a small fire which was quickly extinguished. No one was hurt in the attack. Afterwards, the medical team went ashore and the captain, anxious to surrender, ordered white sheets to be draped over the ship's side and the lifeboats to be made ready for a speedy departure.

The second attack was delivered by nine Typhoons of No 198 Squadron. They were led by Group Captain Johnny Baldwin, who also commanded No. 123 Wing. The attack was directed against two vessels, a large three-funnel liner and a smaller ship moored nearby. It was devastatingly successful. Some forty rockets struck the bigger vessel, the 60lb warheads penetrating her hull to explode inside. She was soon ablaze from stem to stern. Thirty more rockets hit the smaller ship, which developed a heavy list and began to sink, belching smoke.

The third attack was made by No. 263 Squadron. Once again, the *Deutschland* was the target. As the Typhoons began their attack run her crew scrambled into the lifeboats and made for the shore, unharmed. The *Deutschland* was set on fire and was sunk a few minutes later by the bombs of No. 197 Squadron's Typhoons.

The RAF pilots headed back to their bases in Holland and Belgium. The next day, British forces occupied the port of Lübeck, and it was only then that the full tragedy of what had occurred was revealed. The ships had been filled to capacity, not with German troops being evacuated to Norway, but with thousands of former concentration camp inmates.

As the war in Europe approached its inevitable end, orders had been issued by *Reichsführer* Heinrich Himmler, head of the SS, that no concentration camp inmates were to be allowed to fall into Allied hands. Those who could still march were to be moved away from the Allied line of advance; the remainder were to be killed. At Neuengamme, near

Hamburg, where half the prisoners were either Russians or Poles, 1000 were murdered immediately. Many of the 20,000 others were quickly dispersed, but several thousand more were herded into Lübeck during the last days of April. Some 2300 were crammed into a 1936-ton freighter, the *Athen*, whose captain was threatened with death by the SS guards if he did not cooperate, and were then ferried to a three-funnel liner. She was the 27,561-ton *Cap Arkona*.

Before the war she had been known as the Queen of the South Atlantic, carrying out luxury cruises between Hamburg and Rio de Janeiro. Her captain, Heinrich Bertam, defied the SS for a whole day, but in the end an SS officer arrived bearing an order for his execution if he did not comply. Bertram was left with no alternative, and over the next four days about 7000 prisoners from Neuengamme were packed like sardines into the liner, a vessel with accommodation and sanitary arrangements for only 700 people in her wartime role as a troopship. In addition to the prisoners, 500 SS guards also went aboard.

Meanwhile, 3000 more prisoners had been loaded on to another vessel, the 2815-ton freighter *Thielbeck*. On both vessels, the prisoners were battened down for days in darkness and stinking squalor, half dead already from starvation. In addition, two large barges were filled with several hundred men, women and children from the camp at Stutthof. On 2 May, a transfer of prisoners took place between the *Cap Arkona*, the *Thielbeck* and the *Athen*. On the following morning, 4150 remained on the liner and 2750 on the *Thielbeck*. Another 2000 were on the *Athen*, whose captain decided to return to port. The SS guards protested, but according to some accounts were overwhelmed by the ship's crew. The vessel put into Neustadt, and one of the survivors, Mikelis Mezmalietis, recalled what happened next.

> *On the morning of 3 May there was a terrible explosion. After a short time one of the stronger prisoners who had been aloft ran down to tell us that the Americans (sic) had bombed the Cap Arkona and sunk it. Everyone who could move got very excited and tried to get to the one exit. In a moment we felt the ship starting to move fast, and then it stopped.*
>
> *Nobody spoke for an hour. Then all those who could, got up and ran out, especially the German crew; we had arrived at Neustadt. I was unable to move, and was left for dead. After perhaps another hour I crawled on all fours up to the top deck . . .*
>
> *That afternoon two strong young prisoners boarded the ship to see what they could take. They were not from my ship; they turned out to be French students. They were very surprised to see me; they went searching for other prisoners but found none. Then they carried me from the ship and took me*

*to the barracks at Neustadt, where they washed me and put me to bed in a
spare bed in their room.*

The other prisoners who got away from the *Athen* eventually made
contact with advance patrols of the British Army. They were the lucky
ones.

On board the stricken, blazing *Cap Arkona*, more than 4000 prisoners
were burning to death or suffocating in the smoke. A few managed to
break out and jump into the sea, where they were picked up by trawlers.
More – about 350 in all, many suffering from burns – managed to escape
before the liner capsized and swam ashore, only to be shot and clubbed
to death by SS troops and fanatical Hitler Youth members.

Of the 2750 prisoners on the *Thielbeck*, only about fifty managed to
struggle ashore. Most of them met the same fate as the survivors of the
Cap Arkona. There is no record of how the hundreds of prisoners in
the two barges met their fate. When the British arrived, they found the
barges stranded on the shore. The beaches were littered with dead. The
adults had been shot, the children clubbed to death with rifle butts.

One of the first senior British officers on the scene was Brigadier Derek
Mills-Roberts, commanding No 1 Commando Brigade. While he was at
the scene of the slaughter, Field Marshal Erhard Milch, the former
Luftwaffe general who had been sacked from his post and later made
responsible for the deportation of forced labourers, came to surrender to
him. Milch gave a Nazi salute, his field marshal's baton in his
outstretched hand. The British brigadier snatched it from him and broke
it over his head.

The man responsible for the massacre, Max Pauly – the commandant
of the Neuengamme concentration camp – was later tried as a war crim-
inal in Hamburg and hanged, together with several of his subordinates.
That should have been the end of the *Cap Arkona* affair; unfortunately, it
was not. Nearly forty years after the event, a series of sensational articles
in the West German press claimed that the true facts behind the sinking
of the *Cap Arkona* and the *Thielbeck* had been shrouded in mystery and
secrecy for four decades. One of the claims was that British Intelligence
had known that the vessels were packed with concentration camp
inmates and had done nothing about it. Another was that the RAF,
knowing who the ships carried, had deliberately allowed them to be
attacked in order to give pilots fresh out from England some operational
experience before the war ended.

Such claims were nonsense. In fact, the British had issued clear warnings that all shipping in the Baltic would be subject to air attack, unless
vessels displayed prominent Red Cross markings. None of the vessels

Right to the end, the RAF harried German shipping in the Baltic with its fighter-bombers, inflicting enormous damage. (RAF)

involved carried such markings, and the RAF had no reason to believe that they were carrying anything other than troops – and perhaps members of the Nazi leadership – to sanctuary in Norway.

Elsewhere, the desperate last-minute evacuations continued. Between 1 and 8 May, small craft and naval ferry barges of the 13th Landing Flotilla uplifted around 150,000 refugees and troops from the landing stages of the lower Vistula to Hela, from where the transports *Sachsenwald* and *Weserstrom* and the torpedo boats T36 and T108 evacuated the first 8850 on 3 May. Following the surrender of German forces in north-west Germany and Denmark, the freighters *Linz, Ceuta, Pompeji* and the auxiliary cruiser *Hansa*, which were outside territorial waters at the time, proceeded to Hela on 5 May with the destroyers *Hans Lody, Friedrich Ihn, Theodore Riedel* and the torpedo boats T17, T19, T23, T28 and T35. These vessels, together with a number of minesweepers and training ships, embarked 45,000 refugees and sailed for Copenhagen, beating off attacks by Soviet torpedo-boats operating out of Kolberg on the way.

Arriving at Copenhagen on 6 May, the fast warships were unloaded in the roads in order to achieve a rapid turnround. On 7 May, the destroyers *Karl Galster, Friedrich Ihn, Hans Lody, Theodore Riedel* and Z25, together with the torpedo boats T17, T19, T23 and T28, joined now by the destroyers Z38 and Z39 and the torpedo boat T33 from Swinemünde, put into Hela once more and took off 20,000 soldiers and refugees, who were disembarked at Glücksburg on 9 May, the day after the surrender of all German forces came into effect. A further 5730 refugees were taken off by the freighters *Weserberg* and *Paloma*, and 1500 by the small steamer *Rugard*, which evaded attempts by three Soviet torpedo boats to capture her on 8 May.

In all, between 25 January and 8 May 1945, 1,420,000 refugees were evacuated by sea from the Gulf of Danzig and Pomerania. This is a recorded figure; to it must be added some 600,000 more, evacuated over shorter distances a step ahead of the advancing Russians.

It was not quite the end. On 8 May, sixty-five small craft of the German Navy set out from Libau, heading west and carrying 14,400 troops and refugees; while sixty-one similar craft set out from Windau, carrying 11,300 troops. The next day, some of the slower craft were intercepted by Soviet warships, but only 300 persons went into captivity to join the 200,000 left behind in Kurland.

CHAPTER EIGHTEEN

Aftermath

On 6 May, 1945, a British naval force comprising the cruisers *Birmingham* and *Dido* and the destroyers *Zealous, Zephyr, Zest* and *Zodiac* sailed from England, passed through the German mine barrages off the Skagerrak and arrived at Copenhagen on 9 May, where the cruisers *Prinz Eugen* and *Nürnberg* – the only major units of the *Kriegsmarine* still afloat – were surrendered by Vice-Admiral Wilhelm Meendsen-Bohlken, the last commander of the German surface fleet. Command of all German naval units was now assumed by Vice-Admiral Reginald Vesey-Holt, the newly-appointed Flag Officer Denmark. The takeover operation was covered by a task force under Vice-Admiral Rhoderick McGrigor; it comprised the escort carriers *Searcher* and *Trumpeter,* the cruiser *Norfolk* and the destroyers *Carysfort, Zambesi, Obedient, Opportune* and *Orwell.*

Later in the month, the *Prinz Eugen* and *Nürnberg* were escorted to Wilhelmshaven by British destroyers, where they remained to await disposal. The *Nürnberg* was ceded to the Soviet Union, and in January 1946 she sailed to Libau, where she was handed over to the Russians. Renamed the *Admiral Makarov*, she served with the Baltic Fleet until at least 1953, being scrapped sometime in the following years.

An altogether grimmer fate awaited the *Prinz Eugen*, although before finally meeting it she showed a remarkable capacity for survival. Ceded to the United States, she sailed for Boston with a mixed crew of Americans and Germans in 1946, and in March she passed through the Panama Canal to San Diego, where the last German crew members left the ship. In May she sailed for Bikini in the Marshall Islands, where she was to act as a target vessel in America's first post-war atomic bomb tests. At 0900 on 1 July, 1946, during the 'Able' series of tests, an atomic bomb dropped by a B-29 bomber detonated at just over 500 feet above the fleet of target ships. *Prinz Eugen*, moored 1194 yards away from the point of the explosion, survived the test undamaged.

On 25 July 1946, during test 'Baker', she was subjected to an underwater atomic test at a range of 1990 yards. Again, she survived with no apparent structural damage, but she was heavily contaminated by radioactivity. Towed to Kwajalein Atoll, she was decommissioned on 29 August 1946 and plans were made to use her as a naval torpedo and gunnery target. On 21 December that year, she took on a 35-degree list to starboard as a result of minor damage sustained to her stern. Salvage crews could not be brought in, but she was towed to Enubuj Reef, where she capsized the next day.

The US government refused to allow her to be scrapped because of the danger that her radioactive steel might enter the world market, and she lies there still, with the exception of her twelve-ton port propeller, which was removed in 1978 at the request of former crew members after due permission had been obtained and now stands as a memorial near Kiel.

Of the other major warships that had fought in the Baltic, the *Admiral Scheer*, capsized by RAF 'Tallboy' bombs at Kiel on 9 April 1945, was partially scrapped and the remains buried under rubble when the basin was filled in to make a new quay after the war. Her sister ship, the *Lützow*, also crippled by 'Tallboys', lay where she was beached at Swinemünde until the 1960s, when she was broken up. The hulk of the battlecruiser *Gneisenau*, remained where she had been sunk as a blockship in Gdynia harbour until 1947, when work began on breaking her up; her sister ship *Scharnhorst*, battered to a flaming hulk off Norway's North Cape by the Royal Navy, had gone down on 26 December, 1943.

The heavy cruiser *Admiral Hipper*, heavily damaged by RAF bombing while in dry dock at Kiel in April 1945, was scuttled by explosive charges on 2 May. Refloated in 1946, she was towed to Heikendorf Bay, where she was broken up in 1948-49.

The fate of the light cruiser *Nürnberg* has already been described. Of the others, *Leipzig*, patched up and thrown into the last Baltic battle, served as an accommodation ship for the German Minesweeping Administratioin after the war. On 20 July 1946, she was sunk in the North Sea, laden with poison gas shells. The light cruiser *Köln*, which had been used as a training ship in the Baltic, was heavily damaged by the RAF during a refit at Wilhelmshaven on 3 March 1945, settling on the bottom with her superstructure above water. She was scrapped in 1946.

And the *Emden,* whose last duty had been to bear the coffins of Field Marshal Hindenburg and his wife from the Tannenberg Memorial, was heavily damaged by RAF bombing at Kiel, and scuttled at Heikendorf Bay on 3 May 1945. The wreck was broken up on the spot in 1949.

The aircraft carrier *Graf Zeppelin*, partly complete and scuttled by the Germans at Stettin in January 1945, was raided by the Russians in 1946, and on 7 April 1947 she was taken under tow to Leningrad, her flight deck laden with war booty. Later, she was towed out into the Baltic and used as a floating target for Soviet warships and aircraft in August 1947. The wreck was located in the Southern Baltic in 2006.

In the Baltic states, which had suffered heavily during the war and which soon began to feel the effects of Soviet repression, fighting continued. As Stalinist repressions intensified, more than 170,000 residents of Latvia, Lithuania and Estonia took to the forests to hide from the authorities; many were militia and former SS personnel, who formed themselves into guerrilla bands known as the 'Forest Brothers'. The insurgents ranged from individuals, armed for their own protection, to large and well-organised groups capable of engaging Soviet forces in battle.

During the late 1940s, the guerrillas began to receive increasing help from the British Secret Intelligence Service and the US Central Intelligence Agency. The British effort was code-named Operation *Jungle*, a programme that involved the clandestine insertion of agents into the Baltic states between 1948 and 1955. The agents were mostly Estonian, Latvian and Lithuanian emigrants who had been trained in the UK and were to link up with the anti-Soviet resistance in the occupied states.

The agents were transported by the 'British Baltic Fishery Protection Service (BBFPS)', a covert organisation that used high-speed German S-boats (crewed by former *Kriegsmarine* personnel) launched from harbours in the British Zone of Occupation in northern Germany to spy on the Soviet Navy in the Baltic Sea. Agents were inserted into Palanga, Lithuania; Uzava and Ventspils, Latvia; Saaremaa, Estonia; and Ustka, Poland, all typically via the Danish island of Bornholm, where the final radio signal was given from London for the boats to enter the territorial waters claimed by the USSR. The boats proceeded to their final destinations (typically several miles offshore and known only to the vessels' commanders) under cover of darkness and met with shore parties in dinghies. Returning British agents were received at some of these rendezvous points.

The operation was severely compromised by Soviet counter-intelligence, primarily through information provided by British double agents, notably Kim Philby. In an extensive counter-operation code-named 'Lursen-S' (named for Lürssen, the manufacturer of the E-boats), the NKVD/KGB captured nearly every one of the forty-two Baltic agents inserted into the field. Many of them were turned as double agents who infiltrated and significantly weakened the Baltic resistance movement.

The guerrilla movement was best organised in Lithuania, where guerrilla units were effectively able to control whole regions of the countryside until 1949. When not in direct armed confrontation with the Soviet Army or special NKVD units, they significantly delayed the consolidation of Soviet rule through ambush, sabotage, assassination of local Communist activists and officials, freeing imprisoned guerillas, and printing underground newspapers. Captured Lithuanian Forest Brothers themselves often faced torture and summary execution while their relatives faced deportation to Gulags. Reprisals against collaborators' farms and villages were harsh. The NKVD units, named People's Defence Platoons, used shock tactics; the corpses of executed guerrillas, for example, would be publicly displayed in village squares.

By the early 1950s, the Soviet forces had gained the upper hand in the fight against the Forest Brothers. Intelligence gathered by the Soviet spies in the West and KGB infiltrators within the resistance movement, in combination with large scale Communist mop-up operations in 1952, cleared most of the last remaining guerrilla fighters, and those that remained laid down their arms in response to a Russian amnesty following Stalin's death in 1953, although isolated engagements continued into the 1960s. A small number of guerrillas remained in hiding until the 1980s, by which time the independence of the Baltic States from Soviet domination was on the horizon.

In Estonia, particularly around the strongholds held by the SS formations in the closing months of the war, a deadly legacy remains in the form of hundreds of unexploded bombs and shells which are unearthed every year and which must be dealt with by the country's bomb disposal squads. Here, the Second World War continues to claim lives.

In Eastern Europe, the war had utterly destroyed what had hitherto been the keystone of society – the nation-state, where sovereign governments had ruled over a clearly defined territorial area, framing laws and ensuring obedience to them, providing protection for property, and permitting the development of industry and trade. Ironically, the destruction of the nation-state in the east had been assisted by the fact that it was in this area, for a variety of reasons, that the adhesive that held such states together had been weakest. The great plains of north-eastern Europe had never lent themselves geographically to the establishment of clearly-defined boundaries; the architects of the Treaty of Versailles in 1919 had made a creditable attempt to fix a boundary between Germany and Poland based on ethnic lines, with due regard for minorities and plebiscites; and yet it was here, over the Polish Corridor and Danzig, that the seeds of the Second World War had taken root.

In the immediate aftermath of the war, it was the Soviet Union, which had suffered the most, that demanded the most massive concessions. The annexation of Latvia, Estonia and Lithuania, and their incorporation into the framework of the Soviet Socialist Republics, ensured Russian domination of the Baltic area for years to come. The whole of Poland was moved westwards to the Oder, extending south from Stettin, now renamed Szcezin; the Soviet Union acquired part of East Prussia and Königsberg, now renamed Kaliningrad; some German territory became Polish; and east Germany was occupied by Russia.

This movement of frontiers, together with the establishment of Communist domination over the whole of north-eastern Europe, created the biggest addition to the stream of refugees who had already been uprooted from their homes by the war and by the liberated inmates of concentration camps. In the latter half of 1945 they could be seen trudging along the roads of Germany, not only homeless but also stateless. Long after some form of order had been superimposed on the ruins of Europe, the remnant of this mass of people still remained, institutionalised, in displaced persons' camps.

The year 1946 saw mass deportations of Germans, at least twelve million of them, from the lands of eastern Europe that had now come under Soviet control. The remnants of the German population of Lithuania were put on deportation trains; ethnic Lithuanians from overcrowded villages took over former German property in Memel, which was now renamed Klaipeda.

Of the millions of Germans caught up in the mass deportations, according to some estimates, three million perished during the process, the victims of starvation, exhaustion, and in many cases brutality. In addion, over a quarter of a million are believed to have died in Soviet labour camps.

In the early years of what came to be termed the Cold War, the Baltic quickly assumed great importance in Soviet strategic planning. Soviet force in this area continued to be built around the Red Banner Baltic Fleet, its principal bases at Kronstadt, Paldiski near Tallinn in Estonia, Riga and Liepaja (the old Libau) in Latvia, and Klaipeda in Lithuania. Its headquarters were at Baltiysk, near what was now Kaliningrad in an annexed corner of the old East Prussia.

In contrast to other areas of the former Reich occupied by the Russians, repair and restoration work on port facilities proceeded with top priority. The Baltic Fleet was based closer to the Soviet heartland than any other, and eventually contained about sixty per cent of the entire dockyard facilities of the Soviet Union. The yards at Leningrad and Kaliningrad became by far the most important of the Soviet establishments for building and repairing surface warships, and the lavish basing facilities in the Baltic later supported many of the tenders and fleet auxiliaries which in turn supported the Soviet battle groups on the high seas when the Russians were finally able to deploy a true 'blue water' fleet in the 1960s.

On the western side of the Baltic, Sweden remained neutral, although in the light of the increasingly powerful Soviet presence on the opposite shore she went to great lengths in the post-war years to modernise and expand her armed forces. In 1948, conscious of the importance of the Baltic in the future strategic planning of the two emerging power blocs, she put forward a proposal for a Scandinavian defence union. The Danish government showed considerable enthusiasm for the idea, but the Norwegians, aware that their geography belonged as much to the North Atlantic as Scandinavia, elected to join the Atlantic Alliance, soon to become NATO.

There remained Finland. Finland had never been a formal ally of Germany, although she had fought as a co-belligerent during the so-called 'Continuation War' of 1941-44. At the end of it, she had been compelled to forfeit Petsamo (Pechenga), Finland's last corridor to the Arctic, with its valuable reserves of nickel; the ground that was relinquished in Karelia included Vyborg, the second city in Finland, along with important harbours, hydroelectric plants, and the papermills and sawmills of the Vuoksi industrial complex.

In 1947, the multi-national Treaty of Paris imposed military restrictions on Finland, limiting the army to a strength of 34,400, the navy to 4500 men and 10,000 tons of shipping, and the air force to 3000 personnel and sixty combat aircraft. Offensive weapons such as bombers, submarines and missiles were forbidden, although in 1963 the conditions were modified to allow the Finns to acquire air defence missiles.

In 1948, Finland and the Soviet Union signed a bilateral Treaty of Friendship, Co-operation and Mutual Assistance. From the military viewpoint, one of the most important clauses ran:

> In the eventuality of Finland, or the Soviet Union through Finnish territory, becoming the object of an armed attack by Germany or any state allied with the latter, Finland will, true to her obligations as an independent state, fight to repel the attack. Finland will in such cases use all her available forces to defend her territorial integrity by land, sea and air and will do so within the frontiers of Finland in accordance with the obligatioins defined in the present agreement and, if necessary, with the assistance of, or jointly with, the Soviet Union.

The treaty was supposed to last for ten years; in the event, it lasted for forty, lapsing only with the disintegration of the Soviet Union.

Soviet North-western Front – Order of Battle, 22 June 1941

COMMANDER: GENERAL F.I. KUZNETSOV

Eighth Army
Commander: General P.P. Sobennikov
10th Rifle Corps
   10th RifleDivision
   48th Rifle Division
   90th Rifle Division
11th Infantry Corps
   11th Rifle Division
   125th Rifle Division
12th Mechanised Corps
   23rd Armoured Division
   28th Armoured Division
   202nd Mechanised Division
   10th Motorcycle Regiment
9th Anti-Tank Artillery Brigade
47th Corps Artillery Regiment
51st Corps Artillery Regiment
73rd Corps Artillery Regiment
39th Anti-Aircraft Artillery Battalion
242nd Anti-Aircraft Artillery Battalion
25th Engineer Regiment

Eleventh Army
Commander: V.I. Morozov
16th Rifle Corps
   5th Rifle Division
   33rd Rifle Division
   188th Rifle Division
29th Rifle Corps
   179th Rifle Division
   184th Rifle Division
3rd Mechanised Corps
   2nd Armoured Division
   5th Armoured Division
   84th Mechanised Division
   5th Motorcycle Regiment
   10th Anti-Tank Artillery Brigade
   270th Corps Artillery Regiment
   448th Corps Artillery Regiment
   615th Corps Artillery Regiment
   110th Howitzer Artillery Regiment
   429th Howitzer Artillery Regiment
   19th Anti-Aircraft Artillery Battalion
   247th Anti-Aircraft Artillery Battalion
In reserve:
   23rd Rifle Division
   126th Rifle Division
   128th Rifle Division

Twenty-Seventh Army
Commander: General N.E. Berzarin
22nd Rifle Corps
   180th Rifle Division
   182nd Rifle Division
24th Rifle Corps
   181st Rifle Division
   183rd Rifle Division
   613th Corps Artillery Regiment
   614th Corps Artillery Regiment
   103rd Anti-Aircraft Artillery Battalion
   111th Anti-Aircraft Artillery Battalion
In Reserve:
   16th Rifle Division
   67th Rifle Division

Soviet Air Force, North-western Front
Commander: General L.P.Ionov
Eight Fighter Aviation Regiments
Eight Bomber Aviation Regiments
Two Assault Aviation Regiments
Nine Artillery Observation Regiments
One Air Reconnaissance Regiment

Bibliography

Anon. Einen Bessern Findst Du Nicht. Kinder-Verlag, 1952.

Bekker, Cajus. The *Luftwaffe* War Diaries. Macdonald, 1966.

Clark, Alan. Barbarossa. Hutchinson 1965.

Compton-Hall, Richard. The Underwater War. Blandford Press, 1982.

Fedeyev, Aleksandr. Leningrad in the Days of the Blockade. Hutchinson, 1946.

Gallagher, Matthew. The Soviet History of World War II. Praeger 1963.

Goure, Leon. The Siege of Leningrad. Oxford University Press 1962.

Haape, Heinrich. Moscow Tram Stop. Collins, 1957.

Jackson, Robert. Air Heroes of World War Two. Arthur Barker, 1978.

Jackson, Robert. The Red Falcons: Soviet Air Force in Action, 1918-1969. Clifton Books, 1969.

Kaberov, Igor. Swastika in the Gunsight. Sutton Publishing, 1999.

Karasev, A. Leningradtsy v Gody Blokady. Moscow State Publishing House, 1959.

Middlebrook, Martin and Everitt, Chris. The Bomber Command War Diaries. Viking, 1985.

Orgill, Douglas. T34: Russian Armour. Macdonald, 1971.

Pavlov, Dmitri V. Leningrad 1941: The Blockade. University of Chicago Press 1965.

Rohwer, J. and Hummelchen, G. Chronology of the War at Sea 1939-45. (2 vols). Ian Allan, 1972.

Thorwald, Jurgen. Flight in the Winter. Hutchinson, 1953.

Toland, John. The Last 100 Days. Random House, 1966.

Wagner, Ray (Ed). The Soviet Air Force in World War II. Doubleday, 1973.

Werth, Alexander. Russia at War. E.P. Dutton, 1964.

Wykes, Alan. The Siege of Leningrad. Macdonald, 1969.

Ziemke, Earl F. Battle for Berlin. Macdonald, 1968.

Ziemke, Earl F. Stalingrad to Berlin: the German Defeat in the East. Government Printing Office, Washington DC, 1968.

Index